# TRUE WITCH

Since its reemergence in the 1950s, Wicca has other high magical practices. Much of the t Familiar lore) has been overlooked in favor of occasionally rigid ceremonialism. On the other end of the spectrum, the Craft has been influenced by New Age concepts, again never really hitting the mark on drawing out ancient wisdom or true Witch power.

*The Once Unknown Familiar* represents a new look at Witchcraft as a whole, presenting it as one of the major shamanic systems of Northern and Western Europe. It focuses on the traditional shamanic means of raising power and synthesizes them into modern Craft work.

In other tribal cultures, both ancient and extant, the power of the shaman is largely bound up in the animal spirit. The Witches too had these animal helpers, but when the Craft was forced underground, many of the myths, legends, and powers surrounding the Familiar were lost. In this text, Timothy Roderick examines many of these tribal cultures to help piece together the probable face of the Familiar, both in its physical and spiritual manifestation.

The information in this book may well change many of the practices of future generations of Witches.

\* \* \*

*"The concept of the 'unknown familiar' becomes an intriguing mystery."*
—**Lynn Andrews**
**author of *Medicine Woman***

*"I particularly liked the section in which he lists the various animal powers—I came away wishing I had a little more "bat" energy in my life. Maybe if I put some time into Tim's suggestions for journal work, I'll find myself flying at night."*
—**Eloise Klein Healy**
**author of *Artemis in Echo Park***

*"At last, a book in honor of the animal kingdom from the witch's perspective.* The Once Unknown Familiar *is a great teacher for contacting your personal familiar and unleashing your hidden animal power, as well as a refresher course for those practitioners who've forgotten the importance of this kingdom."*
—**Kisma Stepanich**
**author of *The Gaia Tradition***

*"... I really have to say that this is certainly the best how-to book on this subject."*
—**Allyn Wolfe**
**Editor of *Red Garters International***
**(Official publication of the New Wiccan Church)**

## ABOUT THE AUTHOR

Timothy Roderick holds a Master's degree in Clinical Psychology. Active in the Transpersonal Psychology movement, Timothy lectures on Pagan spirituality and contemporary culture at various Southern California colleges. He also circles with Earthdance, a Los Angeles coven, which strives to foster awareness of Wicca through workshops and open rituals.

## TO WRITE TO THE AUTHOR

If you wish to contact the author or would like more information about this book, please write to the author in care of Llewellyn Worldwide and we will forward your request. Both the author and publisher appreciate hearing from you and learning of your enjoyment of this book and how it has helped you. Llewellyn Worldwide cannot guarantee that every letter written to the author can be answered, but all will be forwarded. Please write to:

Timothy Roderick
c/o Llewellyn Worldwide
P.O. Box 64383-439, St. Paul, MN 55164-0383, U.S.A.

Please enclose a self-addressed, stamped envelope for reply, or $1.00 to cover costs. If outside U.S.A., enclose international postal reply coupon.

## FREE CATALOG FROM LLEWELLYN

For more than 90 years Llewellyn has brought its readers knowledge in the fields of metaphysics and human potential. Learn about the newest books in spiritual guidance, natural healing, astrology, occult philosophy and more. Enjoy book reviews, new age articles, a calendar of events, plus current advertised products and services. To get your free copy of *Llewellyn's New Worlds of Mind and Spirit*, send your name and address to:

*Llewellyn's New Worlds of Mind and Spirit*
P.O. Box 64383-439, St. Paul, MN 55164-0383, U.S.A.

# The
# ONCE
# UNKNOWN
## *familiar*

*Shamanic Paths to Unleash*
*Your Animal Powers*

## TIMOTHY RODERICK

1994
Llewellyn Publications
St. Paul, Minnesota 55164-0383, U.S.A.

FIRST EDITION
Second Printing, 1994

Section illustrations by Joe Krejci

Library of Congress Cataloging in Publication Data

Roderick, Timothy, 1963–
    The once unknown familiar : shamanic paths to unleash your animal
powers / Timothy Roderick.
        p.    cm.
    Includes bibliographical references.
    ISBN 0–87542–439–2 (pbk.) : $10.00
    1. Familiars (Spirits)    2. Spiritual life.    I. Title.
    BF1557.R63    1994
    133.4'3—dc20                                                94–5748
                                                                        CIP

Llewellyn Publications
A Division of Llewellyn Worldwide, Ltd.
P.O. Box 64383, St. Paul, MN 55164-0383

*To Bea, the once unknown inspiration.*

# ACKNOWLEDGEMENTS

Many people have aided in the creation of this book. Undoubtedly, the most influential has been my editor and good friend Mead Hunter. Without his skill and sensitivity this book would have never come to light.

I would also like to thank the following people who helped in the creation of this manuscript: Joe Krejci, who kept on believing in this project; Cathy Ida, who unquestioningly helped in the acquisition of certain reference materials; Laurie J. Marks, who encouraged me to write, as did the many people who attended the 1990 Gardnerian Pacific Lammas Gather; the past and present members of Earth Dance; Judith Malinzak, who kept me grounded and my thoughts in perspective; Varda of Crescent's Shadow, who gently questioned everything; Morven Forest and Dr. Elior Kinarthy, who nurtured my growth as a teacher. Finally, thanks to G.L.C., who provided the creative atmosphere, time, resources, and loving support with which to manifest this book.

# CONTENTS

# SECTION 1

## on familiar ground

# un-familiar surroundings

When you see the kingdom spread upon the earth, the old way of living in the world is annihilated. That is the end of the world. The end of the world is not an event to come, it is an event of psychological transformation, of visionary transformation.

— Joseph Campbell, *The Power of Myth*[1]

What is a Familiar? Ask any child and the answer you may expect is, "It's the black cat that rides on the end of a Witch's broom!" Ask adults, and they will look at you very oddly—and then answer just as their children did. But if you ask the ones who call themselves Witches, you'll get a wide variety of responses: "It's any animal with which I have a psychic connection"; "Familiars help with magic"; "Familiars are always wild animals"; or even, "Familiars are spirits." The modern craft of the Witch, because it is reconstructed from sometimes half-forgotten lore and myth, encourages such a variety of opinion; indeed, because Witchcraft is a constantly evolving discipline, it thrives on it. Before the Familiar can really be defined, then, we need a clearer image of the Familiar's spiritual collaborator: the Witch.

First and foremost, a Witch is a shaman. What does this slippery term signify in relation to the modern magical practitioner? Shamanism is difficult to define; most anthropological scholars dodge defining it at all. Through the occasional definitions I ran across, I began to understand the pattern exhibited by most shamans, and through my own experience a definition began to emerge. Through this definition, I realized that the Witch really is a shaman after all.

Modern Wicca, of course, is said to originate from Northern and Western Europe; and when one thinks of the shamans of Europe, one usually tends to think of the organized Bardic tradition, the Druids and mystery schools of sixth-century Britain. However, the way of shamans is not now, nor has it ever been, something that could be learned by attending a school. It is a way that moves the practitioner along a solitary path, yet connects him or her to all.

Shamanism can be defined through both experience and practice. The practices of shamans also comprise the practices of the modern Witch. These practices include midwifery, seercraft, herbalism, healing, counseling, presiding over the traditional rites of passage (such as birth, marriage, and death), and of course magic. But more important than the crafts is the experience of the shaman.

The activity of the shaman centers around uniquely experiencing the Gods. What makes shamans different from other magical, religious, or spiritual folk is their ability to directly connect with deity. They know the Goddesses and the Gods in a personal way. They find their Gods everywhere: trees, stones, the Sun, Moon, and stars, and perhaps especially in animals.

Above and beyond their crafts and experiences, however, Witches are themselves symbols, archetypes. They are symbols of all that is wild, liberated, and free in spirit. The name of the Witch's spiritual path is Wicca, which means "craft of the wise," signifying the wisdom one acquires through the experience of this natural wildness.

Our shamanic Witch-ancestors lived in harmony with the forests and other places often considered wasteland by the rest of the community. In these places of enchantment, they learned from the wilderness, the animals, and the plants. Their teachers were the Moon, the Sun, and the stars. They learned from the turnings of the seasons and drew power from these cycles. In spring they witnessed the magic of regeneration and birth; summer taught them of fruition and of the bounty of the Earth, their Mother. In the fall, they learned the mysteries of the harvest, of reaping the first fruits and of giving thanks, while hard winters would show them the passage through death and the promise of rebirth.

Witches felt the vibratory hum of personal power within their own being; they knew that power was not something gained from reading a book or joining a group. Neither were the wild Witches' Gods the gods described by books or groups. Their Gods were, as Joseph Campbell has written, "familiar," personally relevant sources of power based on the archetypes of the ancient Goddesses and Gods, which are the powerful tides of nature: the powers of wind, fire, water, earth, and of course animals.

To date in the modern Witch's tradition, serious thought has rarely gone into incorporating the Familiar into a more important role in the lives of Witches. Familiars are generally thought of as animals kept by a Witch, but there exists little formulation about the Familiar presence beyond this. One can speculate on the reason for this, but the main reason is that those who have taken an active role in the reconstruction of the Wiccan path have routed it away from many of its wild-Witch or shamanic trappings. Much of Wicca as it is practiced today draws on belief systems ranging from ceremonial qabalism to New Age philosophies, but rarely runs true to its original form—namely, the shamanic heritage of Northern and Western Europe.

Once the path of the Witch resumes a shamanic turn, the image of the Familiar begins to take on more meaning. The Familiar is elevated from its role as the friendly household animal to the role reserved by all traditional cultures for the animal helper: guide, source of knowledge and healing.

Since most of what is known about Familiars has been distorted over the centuries by purveyors of mass culture from Pope Innocent VIII to Walt Disney, it is time to dispense with inherited (and therefore unexamined) assumptions and find the truth for ourselves. On this journey, each of us can actively participate in the development of the modern Craft. By examining the customs and magical practices of shamanic, tribal people around the globe, we may find, as did our ancestors, that the place of the Familiar is at the center of our spiritual and magical lives.

## US AMONG THE BEASTS

The contemporary Witch believes in nature as a manifestation of the Divine. The principle deities of Wicca are the Goddess and the God. The Goddess represents all that is divinely feminine in spirit and in nature. Her symbols are the Moon and Earth, and Her cycles reflect the three archetypal stages of womanhood: the Maiden of youth, the Mother of fruition, and the Crone of repose and wisdom. The God represents all that is divinely masculine in spirit and in nature. His symbol is the Sun, which dies and is reborn in its annual cycle across the heavens. He is Lord of the Dance of life. Wherever there is movement, growth, and change, He is there too.

Though these are genuinely archetypal deity figures, for the Witch to fully reclaim his or her European shamanic heritage, an exploration of the older and more primitive notions of deity might be in order. These older images have been mostly non-anthropomorphic—that is, they are not images of a deity in human form. These older figures are those upon which the images of the Goddess and God have been layered. Much of the archaeological data strongly suggests that one of the first notions of a higher power of any kind was in animal form, or zoomorphic.

Scholarship in this area generally concurs that the so-called "chapel" cave paintings uncovered in the last century, such as those of Lascaux and Trois Frères in France, depict the earliest recorded impressions of deity. The cave walls in these chapels are covered with images of animals. Some depict half man-half animal creatures, which are thought to represent shamans at work.

Ancient reverence for the animal world was natural because animals obviously possessed abilities and strengths far beyond those of mere mortals. Slowly, through time, the images of the animal-Gods began to be replaced by human forms.

For the Witch, the animal never lost its place of power after all. Though perhaps animals lost their preeminence, they stayed in the shadows and were known as helping entities. Upon this basis, the idea of the Familiar was born and it has remained in the lore of the Witch for centuries since.

Margaret Murray created a handy categorization of the Familiar in the European tradition. In her book *The Witch-Cult in Western*

*Europe,* Murray pointed out that the Familiar should be regarded in two ways: as the physical Familiar and as the spiritual Familiar, also respectively known as the "domestic" and as the "divining" Familiar. The image of the domestic familiar is not unlike the popular notion of today; that is, it was the animal that a magical worker kept in her or his presence as a tool of powerful magic and as a representation of divinity in nature. The divining Familiar was a spirit-animal that seemed to change with the passage of time.[2] One year the spirit animal would appear to the Witch in the form of a bear; the next year it might appear as a dog. Traditional magical lore is replete with teachings about this spirit-animal aspect of the Familiar. It is this aspect I call the *Familiar Self.*

In the idea of the Familiar Self is the concept that certain animal spirits actually live inside each of us and are formative influences on our individual personalities, lending to each of us special abilities and attributes. For instance, the lion lends us strength and the wolf lends us endurance. The essence of the Familiar Self is that it is the embodiment of our unconscious processes.

And thus our journey begins here, with the Familiar Self.

The belief that the Familiar resides within each of us is nothing new. It was long held as spiritual truth by many magical workers within various stages of historical and religious development. What is significant is the similarities found in otherwise disparate cultures in regard to the Familiar or animal spirit. The belief that the Familiar resided within was basic to ancient Celtic, Siberian, Polynesian, and native North American magical workers,[3] and this idea continues to exist in the beliefs of many "primitive" cultures today. These beliefs include the idea of several souls residing within the same body. Typically within this type of spiritual system, it is believed that each of these souls comprises the total human spirit. Each of these spiritual aspects governs a certain function within the whole soul. One fraction might communicate with the universal forces, while another will satiate the carnal needs for sex, food, shelter, and so forth.

An example of this type of belief appears among the Siberian shamans of the Kets, Khants, and Yukagris. The Kets believe in seven souls which comprise the whole of the human soul; the Khants believe in four, and the Yukagris have three.[4] One of these souls is typically regarded as the personal animal power.

When a tribe sanctifies one particular animal power, this tribe is said to be practicing a totemic belief system. Anthropologically speaking, totemism is believed to be the oldest form of worship. A totem is personified power, usually in the form of an animal, but sometimes the form is plant or mineral. For instance, a tribe that calls itself the "Dog tribe" would have Dog as their totem animal. Dog would be the power of the tribe's people. These same totemic beliefs have also been echoed in the tribal Northern and Western European traditions.

Animal imagery appeared to be a popular theme of Iron Age Celtic art. The sheer number of artifacts with the animal motif indicates a respect for animals far beyond the ordinary. In time the Celtic fascination with animals became the basis of the animal iconography found on the heraldic shields that were so prevalent during the Middle Ages.[5] The heraldic shields that remain today are quaint remembrances of an age when they still stood as symbols of the tribal, totemic customs observed by the early Europeans.

In many tribal cultures, the totem is most often viewed as a symbol of the tribe's cosmology.[6] In these cultures it is believed that humans are descendants of animals in general, and each tribe is a descendant of one specific animal. Actually, the word "totem" is said to mean "related through the mother,"[7] and thus the animal in this mythological construct stands as a representative of the Goddess, the one who gave birth to all. That animal is revered by the members of the tribe, and its magical power is often called upon in the provision of food.

The Venus of Laussel (circa 19,000 BCE), a Goddess bas-relief unearthed in Dordogne, France, is a striking example of this. The artwork is believed to be the oldest image of what is known as "the lady of the beasts," the Goddess who took the form of and gave birth to the animals. She is depicted holding up a crescent bison horn in her right hand while her left hand lays on her womb—connecting the imagery of sacred birth and animals.

Though the animal-totems were sanctified, in many tribes they were hunted and killed as a source of food.[8] When the totem is consumed, every member of the tribe participates in the sacramental meal and thereby assumes the animal's attributes. These cultures literally embrace the pop adage, "you are what you eat." When the totem animal is the sacramental meal, you have before you the origin of those

*Venus of Laussel*

Neolithic bas-relief, c. 19,000 BCE

mythologies that include a God who is slain in order to sustain or redeem the members of a society.

For those within these cultures who are shamans, the wise men and women who confront the world of the supernatural, an animal spirit represents far more than what the rest of the society recognizes in the totem. The shaman, through spiritual work that connects him or her with all of nature, comes to know the animal spirit as a link to the powers of the infinite. The shamans see the Familiar spirit in the role of teacher and guide through the magical world of the unseen.

The Familiar is said to instruct the shaman in the use of its own power. In most traditional cultures, the first reported spiritual experience of a shaman is usually with the animal power. The apprentice must wait for the animal spirit to appear and instruct on how to use its power before this spiritual worker is considered to be magically initiated.[9]

The Shamans of Siberia, for example, believe that each of us has a magical spirit-animal "servant" called the Rekken.[10] The function of the Rekken is to bring whatever the magical worker requests. The magical animal spirits of the Siberian shamans are identical in function to those of the Kahuna masters found thousands of miles away in the Polynesian isles.

In the system of magic called Huna (which literally means "secret"), the animals hold a position of prominence in the shaman's spiritual workings. It is believed that the Familiar Self (the Unihipili) is part of a trinity of souls that comprises the human spirit.[11] The job of the Familiar Self is to help manifest the will of the magical worker.[12]

The Unihipili, just like the Rekken and the totem, is regarded as a personal animal spirit that ventures into the physical world to bring forth the magical worker's wishes. Likewise, this was the task of the Familiar in the European traditions of magic—to work the will of the Witch.[13]

# THE MISSING LINK

The way the Familiar Self experiences and unleashes its power is through our physical bodies. Its expression is nonverbal; emotions, sensations, and body language are its modes of expression, as is the magical expression of the unconscious mind.[14] The two are linked—

the Familiar Self and the unconscious. Or, to put it more succinctly, they are layered in such a way that one aspect is transparent to the other. Both are transparent to spirit.

Shamans have intuited this link between the physical, mental, and spiritual bodies[15] and used this link to create larger, more significant links that extended beyond personal boundaries. The Polynesian Kahuna masters believed that the physical body affected the spiritual, just as the spiritual affected the physical. The Kai of New Guinea believed in a soul-substance which permeated every part of the body.[16]

Many native cultures believe that we are physical and spiritual descendants of the animals, and as such, the animal spirit is thought to be one with our bodies.[17] Australian Aboriginals may identify the animal spirit as a father, brother, or even as synonymous with their own flesh,[18] which potently illustrates how keenly they feel the inextricable connection of spirit and matter.

Likewise, this belief that one world affects the other is fundamental to traditional Wicca; as the old magical saying goes, "as above so below." In other words, the physical body, and all that belongs to the physical realm, affects the spiritual. Of equal importance is how the spiritual affects the physical. The unconscious mind links us to the spiritual side of ourselves. Any communication between the two worlds (or the two minds) is crucial to the workings of magic and transformation.

## ANIMAL TALK

The Familiar Self is the part of us that communicates through symbol. It has the capacity to understand those universal symbols that arise from what Carl Jung referred to as our collective unconscious. These images are depersonalized; they access the taproot of a society and therefore are often seen most vividly through mythologies of ancient cultures. As basic human archetypes, they address experiences common to all of humanity. But the Familiar Self makes these symbols relevant to each of us by personalizing these myths and revealing their symbols in dreams.[19] In this way, the personal mind is linked with the universal mind and the mysteries of the universe, personal growth, and transformation are accessible to all. Of the various ways of establishing communication with the Familiar Self, none is as basic as the symbol system utilized in ritual.

Rituals effectively act as bridges between those layered aspects of spirit and matter and link the conscious to the unconscious mind. A good ritual is constructed from the symbol language of mythology and dream. Outer forms of ritual, such as symbolic gestures or the "smells and bells," address inner issues which, in turn, can trigger communication between the conscious and unconscious Familiar Self. By participating in rituals we speak the not-so-foreign language of myth and open the communication barriers between the aspects of self. Once the channels are open, personal magic and transformation begin to occur, and just like the Witch's animal helpers, the Rekken, the Unihipili, and the totem, the inner Familiar works the Witch's will.

Though the Christian Church did its best to eradicate many of these beliefs among the European folk,[20] vestiges of the understanding of the Familiar's true workings among Witches seemed to have survived as late as the middle 1600s. In 1588 one Essex Witch confessed that her cat "would doe her good seruice, if she would she might send her of her errand. This cat was with her a while, but the weasill and the toad came and offered their good seruice."[21] Another confessed that a "cat came unto her. … The cat bade her not be afraid, she would do her no harm. She had served a dame for five years in Kent, that was now dead, and if she would, she would be her servant."[22] Anne Whittle of Lancaster said that a "spotted bitch" appeared to her, "which then did speak vnto her … and said, that she could haue Golde, Siluer and worldly Wealth at her will."[23] In 1613, Alizon Deuice, also of Lancaster, confessed that a Familiar appeared to her and told her that she could "have and doe what shee would."[24]

Although of course we must look critically at testimony extracted from enforced confessions, there do exist some startling parallels between these accounts of Familiars and the ideas about animal powers existing among both ancient and contemporary magical societies. For instance, the Unihipili was called upon to manifest the shaman's will,[25] the Rekken was called to the same service,[26] and much of the Celtic shaman's power was bound up in the animal helper as well.[27]

Carrying out the duties of the shaman has always been the function of the Familiar Self, according to known magical lore. It seems that tribal wisdom introduced this concept long before the twentieth century, Jung, and the so-called scientific understanding of the unconscious mind. But the news that we have come full circle in accepting the wisdom of primitive lore should be no news to the Witch.

## GETTING STARTED

Occultist Dion Fortune is credited with penning one of the best definitions of magic, calling it "the art of changing consciousness at will."[28] The first step in becoming an adept in changing consciousness is knowing the self. One of the first teachings of the Craft of the Wise is that if you cannot find what you are looking for within yourself, you will never find it elsewhere.[29] To change our consciousness we must first come to terms with our own psyches.

The Familiar Self is a permanent fixture of the psyche, reflecting the personality.[30] By coming to know the animal residing within, we can understand ourselves and other people better. We must become psychic detectives, sacred hunters tracking the footprints of our innermost selves.

Each animal carries with it certain powers and abilities that are bestowed on the bearer of the animal spirit. My Familiar Self is the fox, which makes me playful, stealthy, and optimistic. The gifts the fox gives me are perseverance, the power to avoid danger, and the ability to go unseen. Your Familiar Self as well gives you special abilities that I and others may not possess. Not only that, but your Familiar Self may express itself in ways that others who have the same animal may not.

The basic animal self, the Familiar Self, remains with you through your lifetime. However, when certain abilities are needed or particular ends are desired, we can call up any of the animal spirits to empower our lives. When wisdom is needed, we may invoke the power of the Bear, who is representative of the Goddess force, Mother of the woods and mountains. When foresight is needed, we may invoke the power of the Eagle who climbs the skies, the domain of the Sun, the God Force which evokes strength, foresight, and knowledge.

This is the way of the animal powers—to evoke first-hand knowledge of the energies of the Universal Power, both male and female. When working with Familiars, it becomes apparent that each of their powers is governed by either male, active energy, or by female, nurturing, receptive energy. Neither is greater than the other and both are of equal value in generating magical power. Both could be considered in terms of electrical charges: positive and negative. One without the other is ineffective in creating active energy. We need both to sustain life and create anew. The male and female energies interact in the spiritual dance of eternity which is choreographed in each of our lives.

The time has come to begin your internal journey. The format of this book is primarily that of discussion first and then practical exercises, so journeying to find the Familiar Self will come in stages. Through the early exercises in this workbook, you will discover the nature of your Familiar Self. But first and foremost, you must acknowledge your first steps on the path to the center. You must pass through the process of initiation. In this initiation you will align with the alchemical elements that symbolize the constituents of the life force to the modern Wiccan. By participating in the elemental initiation, you allow their life-giving components to become instilled in the spirit. You cleanse, purify, and generally set the stage for the even deeper, more primal work to follow.

## NOTES

1. Joseph Campbell and Bill Moyers, *The Power of Myth* (New York: Doubleday, 1988), 230.

2. Margaret Murray, *The Witch-Cult in Western Europe* (London: Oxford University Press, 1962), 206–8.

3. Margaret Murray, *The God of the Witches* (New York: Oxford University Press, 1970), 33.

4. Karl H. Schlesier, *The Wolves of Heaven* (trans. *Die Wölfe des Himmels*) (Norman: University of Oklahoma Press, 1987), 28, 29.

5. John Matthews, *Talesin; Shamanism and the Bardic Mysteries in Britain and Ireland* (Hammersmith, England: Aquarian Press, 1991), 155.

6. Monica Sjoo and Barbara Mor, *The Great Cosmic Mother* (San Francisco: Harper Collins, 1987), 79, 80.

7. Sjoo and Mor, 80.

8. Geza Roheim, *The Eternal Ones of the Dream* (New York: International Universities Press, 1945), 130.

9. Max Freedom Long, *Secret Science Behind Miracles* (Marina Del Rey, CA: DeVorss, 1983), 179.

10. Marie Antoinette Czaplicka, *Aboriginal Siberia* (London: Oxford University Press, 1969).

11. Brad Steiger, *Kahuna Magic* (Glouchester, MA: Para Research, Inc., 1981), 18.

12. It was believed that the animal spirit could be directed to create the desired future of the shaman. Long, 168.

13. The various trial records reflect this, as in George Giffard's *Dialogue Concerning Witches*, vol. 8 (London: Percey Society, 1843), 20, and in Thomas Potts' book, *Pott's Discovery of Witches in the County of Lancaster*, vol. 6 (Manchester: Chetham Society, 1745), B5, C.

14. Loretta A. Malandro, Larry Barker, and Deborah Barker, *Nonverbal Communication* (New York: Random House, 1989), 9.

15. See, for example, Long, 15.

16. W.H.R. Rivers, *Medicine, Magic and Religion* (New York: Harcourt and Brace, 1979), 19.

17. James G. Frazer, *Totemism and Exogamy*, vol. 2 (Cambridge: Messrs. Macmillan and Co. Ltd., 1968), 104.

18. Roheim, 130.

19. Joseph Campbell, *The Hero With a Thousand Faces* (New Jersey: Princeton University Press, 1973), 19.

20. See, for example, Starhawk, *Truth or Dare* (San Francisco: Harper and Row, 1987); Riane Eisler, *The Chalice and the Blade* (San Francisco: Harper and Row, 1987); and Sjoo and Mor.

21. Giffard, 20.

22. Giffard, 39–40.

23. Potts, B5.

24. Potts, C.

25. Long, 168.

26. Czaplicka, 172.

27. Matthews, 150.

28. Quoted by Starhawk, *The Spiral Dance: A Rebirth of the Ancient Religion of the Great Goddess* (New York: HarperCollins Publishers, 1989), 7.

29. According to the contemporary adaptations of "The Charge of the Goddess," originally obtained and published in Charles G. Leland's book, *Aradia, Gospel of the Witches* (Washington: Phoenix Publishing, 1990).

30. Frazer, 3:55.

# *meditation and the familiar*

ince the Familiar Self is the animal spirit dwelling within, our starting point in the discovery of the Familiar Self is also within. The most effective way of internal searching is through the ancient discipline of meditation.

Meditation is a technique that can help us readily access our creative, innovative, animal impulses. The Familiar Self is synonymous with the unconscious mind, and during meditation we bring the usually clattering jumble of our conscious minds into a calm focus. We loosen the usually tight grip of the conscious mind processes; in essence, we are able to work with the unconscious mind consciously.

When this happens we gain "magical consciousness." The process of loosening the unconscious mind enables us to draw together fragmented pieces of our lives (events, thoughts, feelings, relationships, etc.) and form whole pictures. We are able to see how the pieces are interrelated and how our lives are linked with the lives of others as well as with the plants and animal life.[1]

Many people, when they first think of meditation, imagine chanting "Om" and sitting in the lotus position for hours. While allied with Eastern traditions of meditation, the Wiccan (i.e., Western) approach is completely different. Western practices tend to use active, guided imagery during meditations in order to transcend the conscious mind, rather than the traditionally Eastern method of repeating a mantra or watching the breath to lull the mind into passivity. Both approaches achieve the same purpose—the preemption of the critical faculties that are the conscious mind's province—but I believe the active approach is more suited to Western consciousness.

## MEDITATION AND MAGIC

As viewed by many of the magical workers native to many societies, meditation is a window into the realm of the mystical. The Bororo shamans of Brazil have sacred "dreams" in their ceremonies of healing and initiation—magical visions, actually, revealed during the enhanced states of perception that accompany meditation. The consciousness is expanded in such states so that the shaman's Familiar Self can communicate through deeply personal symbology. Likewise, the Lapp shamans of Siberia say they enter the terrain of the dread Underworld through an opening in the ground;[2] they journey there to recover the lost Familiar-selves of their patients. They believe that when the "animal power" is lost, an individual is susceptible to physical injury or illness. Symbolically, the opening in the ground through which they spirit-journey represents a deliberately opened hole in the psyche leading to deeper realms. As with the Bororo, the Lapp's journeys are taken on the inner plane, in a trance-like, meditative state.

Meditation is an indispensable part of the aspiring magical worker's spiritual study. Every individual working toward self-discovery through the Familiar Self needs to set aside some special time each day in which to practice meditation and align the personal mind with the cosmic. This period each day should be viewed as "sacred time"; interruptions should either be limited or (preferably) prevented altogether.

The Beginning Exercise that follows this section, like the other meditations in this book, is a guided imagery meditation. In these meditations, you are taken through an internal adventure of sorts, in which the imagery and events are suggested. To help make the experience more vivid and more internally transformative, have a partner read it to you as you close your eyes and experience the journey. If you have no one available to read the text, it would be a good idea to make an audio recording of it beforehand. Background music is fine if it assists you in achieving the desired altered state, but it is not necessary. The words will suffice.

Make sure you are sitting upright and you have your eyes closed. Many beginning students find it's too easy to fall asleep when lying down to meditate! During the meditation, try to keep body movements to a minimum.

The inner realm is the appointed place from where you will begin your journey.

# BEGINNING EXERCISE

Do this exercise at the start of all the meditations given in this book; it is the basis for all of the following, more advanced guided meditations. Practice it at least once a day or until you begin to feel comfortable enough to guide yourself through it without having someone read it to you.

In your first time through the Beginning Meditation, there will be one point at which it will be suggested that you imagine yourself at a favorite natural setting, a resting place. In the later meditations, this will be the point of departure. This will be where you venture into the magical grounds of the Familiar Self.

To begin this exercise, you should find a comfortable sitting posture. You will be in this position for a while, so be sure it feels conducive to the process of imaging.

**Reader:** Find a posture sitting down that is comfortable for you. You will be in this position for a while, so be sure it feels right to begin with.

Close your eyes and scan your body for tension, starting from your feet, working your way up to the head. Release and relax. Allow a warm glow to fill each area with your every breath.

Inhale deeply through your nose and exhale through your mouth and let the exhaled air take on a sound—any sound. Repeat this three more times.

(**Reader** pause. Then say:)

Continue breathing in a deep, natural, rhythmic pattern. With each breath, feel you are allowing your muscles to float. The surface of the Earth can hold you. Allow it.

Begin to relax your muscles slowly, beginning at the top of your head. Allow this relaxation to warm your body as it eases down to your toes. While this feeling moves across you, imagine a golden light enveloping you. This light covers you like a cocoon. After you see this, imagine your stress melting away like butter. Let the tension slide and drip off your body, down through the floor; allow it to dissolve into the Earth, where it is neutralized.

You can clearly see a blue mist beginning to form around your body. It takes the shape of a swirling globe and it begins to lift you. It takes you higher and drifts you into the dream realm where you will begin your sacred journey.

Now the blue mist globe sets you down and begins to dissipate. You find that you are in your favorite natural setting. It might be the woods, or the beach, or a park. It might be near a stream or pond. It is a restful place, and here you can find tranquility and inner strength. Rest now.

(**Reader** pause for a moment.)

It is time to return to the physical world now ... you are returning now to the realm of time and space ... you are here. When you feel that you have fully returned, open your eyes.

Take a moment to recount your experience before answering the journaling questions.

# JOURNALING

As has been stated earlier, this is a workbook. As such, exercises and journaling questions are provided at the end of each section. Take time to answer them.

During the exercise, what was your body positioning? Were you able to relax sufficiently?

What will enable you to relax more fully when you do this meditation again?

How did it feel to have the golden aura surround you?

What was it like to be inside the blue mist that turned into a globe and lifted you?

## ANIMAL OBSERVATION EXERCISE

This exercise is the foundation for many subsequent exercises. For instance, in another chapter you will learn methods of shape-shifting, becoming the Familiar; it is therefore important that you first get a feel for assuming the animal identity. Spend some time repeating this exercise and becoming comfortable with it before moving on to the next chapter and the next set of exercises.

For this exercise, it would be best to go to some natural setting. Find a favorite park, a wooded area, or a beach. For that matter, you could even go to the local zoo. What you really need to find is a place where animals live and can be observed.

Find a spot that is secluded or at least where you will not be disturbed. Close your eyes and, as in the Beginning Exercise, breathe deeply; allow yourself to relax and mentally allow yourself to mentally drift to your favorite place of relaxation. Once you are there, open your eyes once more and let your visual focus center upon an animal. Observe its movements and sounds.

At this point, allow a shift to take place. Imagine yourself where the animal is—mimicking its movements, thinking its thoughts, seeing from its eyes and experiencing life from its senses.

After some time, shift back to your own bodily experience. Take a moment before you answer the following journaling questions.

# JOURNALING

How were the animal's movements different than yours? How were they similar?

What did it feel like to be in the place of that animal?

# A WORD ON YOUR RATE OF PROGRESS

Students of Wicca and magical practices can become impatient about their spiritual growth. Most of us have grown up in a culture that demands immediate results and expects a relatively small amount of work on our part to be the rate of exchange. But microwave spirituality isn't a priority for the Witch. The magical practitioner knows that spiritual growth is a process and—moreover—that this process is its own result. There is no "end of the road" with personal spiritual evolution. Enlightenment finds us before we find it, and the internal rewards of spiritual work are difficult to calculate, weigh, or measure.

Even though we like to set goals for our work in the mundane world, time becomes a less relevant factor in matters of the spirit. The internal changes you will be making along the way need time to seep into the inner core of your being. Undoing years of limited thinking and stripping away layers of dross is an alchemical operation that must be taken at a conservative pace. Transformative magic can be a slow and subtle process, similar to the changing of the seasons.

When exactly did the days of summer become fall? We may mark our calendars and determine the solar position relative to the Earth, but the feelings and energies of autumn are sensed in subtler ways. Similarly, you may barely notice the changes within yourself at first; but one day, suddenly and inexplicably, you will have changed your own spiritual nature.

# JOURNALING

Since working with the Familiar Self on a meaningful level means that I won't have instant results, what can I do to assist the learning process?

Am I really willing to do these things I have just listed? Why or why not?

When I get angry at another person, what animal do I become?

When I am sad, what animal do I become?

What animal do I become when I am happiest?

What are my favorite animals? Choose one of these and use four descriptive words that describe how you feel about that animal or how it makes you feel.

It has been said that people's favorite animals carry features that they feel they themselves possess. Now take a look at the descriptive words about your favorite animal. What are you saying about yourself?

## NOTES

1 . See, for example, Robert Ornstein, *The Psychology of Consciousness* (New York: Viking Penguin Inc., 1986), 199.

2. Joseph Campbell, *The Hero With a Thousand Faces* (New Jersey: Princeton University Press, 1973), 99, 100.

# *initiation*

When you begin something, you initiate. Your work with animals is a beginning on the spiritual path toward discovery of your inner self. Initiations are in essence magical, spiritual births. They are the rites of passage for the Witch or shaman that prepare him or her for the road ahead. Initiations are also celebrations, ways of marking the passage of the seasons of one's internal life.

Usually, magical initiations focus on the symbolism of the Moon.[1] Also typical of magical initiations is the symbolic "death and rebirth" motif. The Moon and the death/rebirth motif correspond naturally, because the Moon appears to "die" as it wanes, yet it is always "reborn" in the course of its 28-day cycle.

Another significant reason why the Moon figures so prominently in the process of initiation is that it is the symbol of the Divine Mother, the Goddess. Physical birth, as the initial entry into physical life, is the first initiation each of us undergoes. Naturally, therefore, we experience spiritual birth through the primary, spiritual Mother, mirroring what happened during physical birth—"as above, so below."

Although ancient in its origins, the initiatory death and rebirth theme can be found in contemporary traditional and magical societies. Among contemporary Northern European traditions, magical initiation rites usually entail a symbolic death and then a re-emergence into a new, spiritually awakened life.[2] Striking similarities in this motif appear throughout the shamanic-magical initiations of the Australian aboriginals and the Native American Pomos of Northern California, as well as in the shamanic rites of the Koryaks, Gilyaks, and Tongas of Siberia.[3] Each in its own way celebrates a cleaving from a material existence and a rebirth into a spiritual one.

## OUR INITIATORY EXPERIENCE

What makes an initiation a directly transformative experience is the fact that it takes place within the psyche. Internal transformation is the ultimate purpose of all ritualized initiations. The initiation process at hand will occur in two stages. First you will align with what are known as the alchemical elements. You will encounter each of the elements on the inner plane. In the process they will suspend the patterns of the conscious mind, thereby facilitating the second part of the initiation— identifying and contacting your Familiar Self.

In the Wiccan tradition, there are four alchemical elements: Air, Fire, Water, and Earth. Alone or in various combinations, these are understood to course through the veins of everything in the universe, both the animate and the apparently inanimate.

Air is any gaseous substance. It is what we breathe; it represents thought, ideas, and all communication.

Fire is any warmth or energy. It is the spark within; it represents internal energy, drive, and force. It is what brought you here to the brink of initiation.

Water is any liquid substance. Water is necessary to all life, and of course the human body consists of at least 96 percent water. Water represents the emotions, cycles, and intuition.

Earth is any solid substance. Earth is the substance of which all things on this planet are made. Earth represents the physical body, mystery, and stability.

Most people have a natural predominance of one or two elements through natal astrological influences, and through the Sun sign in particular: Libra, Gemini, and Aquarius are Airy signs; Aries, Leo, and Sagittarius form the fiery triad; Water rules Cancer, Scorpio, and Pisces; and Taurus, Virgo, and Capricorn represent Earth. Ideally, however, each of us needs to cultivate a full alignment with each of these forces in order to effectively flow with the ever-changing powers of magic.

## ELEMENTS OF LIFE MEDITATION

Follow the imagery of relaxation as outlined in the Beginning Meditation. Once you are fully relaxed, turn on your tape recorder with the meditation below prerecorded. If you have a partner, have the partner begin reading when you are ready.

**Reader**: As a blue mist swirls about your body, you begin to float. You feel yourself being lifted higher as the swirling blue mist becomes a globe around you. It is taking you into the dream realm where you will begin your sacred journey.

The globe of blue mist begins to dissipate, revealing a midnight sky. As the mist clears, you can see that you are in a rocky desert. Brilliant white starlight plays against the black canopy of the desert sky; on the horizon you can see spiny cactus and large boulders. Starlight glitters around their silhouettes.

You can see one very bright star ahead of you, which seems to be guiding or watching over you. This is the North Star, which lives in the place of great wisdom and silence. You turn to your right—the East. A great wind blows the desert sand up into a whirling dervish. The dustdevil approaches you and holds steady a few yards away. Hold your spirit arms up and mentally greet the powers of the East:

> HAIL TO THEE, O MIGHTY WINDS OF THE EAST!
> GUARDIANS OF AIR, KEEPERS OF THE PORTALS OF THE
> FUTURE, GRANT ME KNOWLEDGE AND UNDERSTANDING
> IN THIS, MY SACRED QUEST.

The whirling dervish envelops you. You are now in the center of the swirling air. Feel its power fill you. The dust begins to settle, and the swirl diminishes as you are filled with the power of Air.

Turn now to face the South. There, on the ground before you, is a burning stick. The dancing flame is small at first, but then the flame catches onto other twigs and dried brush. This continues until a ring of flame surrounds you. Hold your arms up and mentally greet the powers of the South:

HAIL TO THEE, O MIGHTY FLAMES OF THE SOUTH! GUARDIANS OF THE POWERS OF FIRE, KEEPERS OF THE POWER TO WILL, GRANT ME STRENGTH OF SPIRIT IN THIS, MY SACRED QUEST.

The flames rise higher; feel their life-giving heat and allow their power to fill you. As you absorb the power of Fire, the flames die down and there is stillness once again. Continuing your circle, face the West. There, a few yards away, is a rushing brook. Hear the soft sound of trickling water rushing over stones. Walk to it and see the stars reflected in its rushing waters.

You step into the brook and suddenly you are up to your waist in water. The water is warm and comforting as it twirls around you. The water begins to rush faster, threatening to pull you under its dark currents. Raise your arms to greet the powers of the West:

HAIL TO THEE, O MIGHTY TORRENTS OF THE WEST! GUARDIANS OF WATER, KEEPERS OF THE PORTALS TO THE PAST, GRANT ME COURAGE IN THIS, MY SACRED QUEST.

Now is the time to absorb the power of Water. As you do so, the level of the brook diminishes until it is only a trickle between your feet. Step out of the stream bed and notice that you are not wet.

Continue your sacred circle: face the North. See the huge, dark stone boulders that lay in a grouping several yards away. Go to them.

You notice that the boulders lay in a circular formation, close together. The only entrance is from the South—a small crevice just big enough to squeeze through. It is very cold within the towering refuge of the stone circle. Moss grows on the inner boulder walls. Carved into the stones are the many faces of your ancient ancestors. Etched in the earth beneath your feet is a spiral, and at its center is a carving of your own face. Hold your arms up, see the North Star, and greet the power of the North:

HAIL TO THEE, O MIGHTY STONES OF THE NORTH! GUARDIANS OF THE EARTH, KEEPERS OF THE POWERS OF SILENCE, GRANT ME WISDOM IN THIS, MY SACRED QUEST.

The ancient wisdom of the North Star is drawn down into your third eye at the center of your brow. The surrounding boulders tremble, then slowly roll apart to allow you passage.

You have been anointed with the elements of life and are centered within your being. You have passed the initiation of elemental alignment.

(**Reader** pause for a moment.)

It is time to return to the physical world now. As you stand in the center of the spiral, allow the blue globe of mist to form and surround you. It is bringing you back to your place of departure. You are returning now. You are here. When you have returned and feel ready, open your eyes. Take a moment to recall your experience before answering the journaling questions.

# JOURNALING

With which elements did you most easily align? Explain the sensations as you passed through these elements.

Which element felt the most foreign to you? Elaborate on your feelings as you passed through this element.

What elements could you ascribe to certain parts of your personality? (Example: I have a very solid, practical way about my dealing with business. I would label this an Earth quality.)

Each of the animal powers is identified with a particular element. For instance, the falcon aligns with Air, the lion with Fire, the hippopotamus aligns with Water and the bear aligns with Earth. Of course, each of us has the natural ability to shape and move the energies of at least one of the elements. We may have noticed this as children; we could make it rain on certain days (natural alignment with Water) or we could cause the wind to blow (natural alignment with Air). Any such native talents are due to inherent connections with elemental powers and, correspondingly, to certain animals aligned with those powers. Note which of the four elements you were able to understand effortlessly, and also note those which felt alien to you. This information should help you in the discovery of your Familiar Self later on.

For now, you need to acquire some facility in aligning with all the elements of life before you can come to terms with the more potent energy form of the Familiar Self. Then the more advanced task of assum-

Air

Fire

Water

Earth

*Animals Identified with the Elements*

Falcon from *Historia Animalum* by Konrad Gesner (Frankfurt, 1585)
Other animals from *The History of Four-footed Beasts and Serpents* by
Edward Topsel (London, 1658)

ing the energies of other Familiar powers will come to you more readily. Take time to repeat the Elements of Life Meditation at least once a day for the next couple of days before moving on to your next work.

# EXERCISE: THE BEASTS

After observing an animal for some time, adopt one of its characteristics, imaginary or real, and incorporate it into your personality for the next 24 hours. By imaginary I mean, for example, that if you saw a bird pecking in the same place for 20 minutes, you might perceive its activity as a sign of tenacity. Whether or not the bird is actually tenacious is irrelevant. Take the perceived trait of the observed animal and incorporate it into your behavior.

# JOURNALING

How did it feel to take on the personality trait of the observed animal?

Was the trait you incorporated foreign to your own traits? How did this affect you?

## NOTES

1. Wendell Beane and William Doty, eds., *Myths, Rites and Symbols: A Mircea Eliade Reader* (New York: Harper/Colophon Books, 1976), 173.

2. Starhawk, *The Spiral Dance: A Rebirth of the Ancient Religion of the Great Goddess* (New York: HarperCollins Publishers, 1989), 160.

3. Beane and Doty, 173.

# finding the familiar

Each one of us has a spirit to wait upon us when we please
to call upon him.
> —Isobel Gowdie (Scottish Witch)[1]

t is here in the second part of the internal or "vision" initiation that the actual hunt for the animal within begins. In cultures where hunting is a life-supporting activity, the imagery and mythology surrounding animals is potent. In many Celtic mythologies, the call from within comes in the shape of an animal who leads the mythic hero into the woods on an adventure to reckon with a mysterious power, or perhaps to come to some high spiritual illumination.[2] For such myths, comparative mythology scholar Joseph Campbell interprets the animal as a representation of the inner call; it is the guide into the netherworld.[3] Carl Jung has similarly characterized the animals that appear in the personal mythic realm of dreams as representing the unconscious, non-human side of our nature. In both cases, the animal leading the adventurer (which is to say, the initiate) into the woods clearly represents a call from deep within, summoning the adventurer into uncharted territory. Using the encoded language of symbol, this deep call exhorts the adventurer to address the issues of the spirit and of the psyche.

> Pwyll, Lord of Dyved ... was in his chief court at Arberth,
> his thoughts and desires turned to hunting.

So begins the tale of Pwyll, Lord of Dyved, as recorded in the medieval Welsh epic, the *Mabinogion*.[4] His story is that of initiation and of descent into the realm of the Familiar Self—the realm of the underworld (another name for the unconscious). In the story, he embarks on a sacred hunt. He encounters magical-looking beasts in the form of dogs that are "glittering, bright white ... and their ears red: the redness of their ears glittered as brightly as the whiteness of their bodies."[5] Directly following his experience with the Familiar beasts, he meets the Lord of the Underworld, and then he undertakes a journey to that realm.

Here, in one of the key Northern European myths,[6] we see the importance of meeting the Familiar Self through the sacred hunt in the magical initiatory process. Finding the Familiar Self in the Welsh case was synonymous with journeying to the underworld, the place that lies between time and space, the place of transformation, magic, and power that lies within each of us. The experience of understanding and acquiring that power, then, is that of the discovery of the Familiar Self.

The hunt theme is echoed in the magical initiation rites in primary cultures globally. To this day, cultures with religio-magic forms of belief expect the magical worker to have his or her first magical experience while meeting the animal-spirit.[7] These may come through a meditation, an experience of magical ecstasy,[8] or even during a hunt for the animal in question.

One of the most intriguing initiations of this last category is that of the Bororo in Brazil. The magical worker, when called by the spirit world to become a shaman, has visions of his Familiar. But the Familiar appears first as a child. The child leads the shaman in a hunt.[9] This hunt inevitably ends with the transfiguration of the child into the animal form which represents the magical worker's power.

The image of the Familiar power, first seen as a child, links once again to the idea that the Familiar Self seems to layer upon the unconscious mind. In popular psychology, it is said that the unconscious houses the "inner child." The Bororo tradition of the metamorphos-

*The Sacred Hunt*

from *The History of Man* by J.W. Buel (Richmond, 1889)

ing Familiar may be an unconscious, synchronistic parallel to the "child" within.

The Familiar Self calls each of us to the ordeal of initiation. We are instinctively drawn to the process as a rite of passage leading us into our full human potential. At the same time, however, the Western mind is taught to value external achievement over internal transformation, so a struggle exists within each of us. We long for the ways of the sacred, but our culture supports the ways of the mundane.

The only remaining refuge comes when we go to sleep each night. The unfulfilled spirit announces through dreams those initiatory images and experiences that are not sought consciously.[10] Sometimes the images come in nightmares. Dream analyst Ann Faraday points out that nightmares are often produced by the unconscious mind to warn us that certain key issues are not being addressed consciously. According to Faraday, animal nightmares are common to those who actively subdue their animal natures and who subsequently begin to lose their natural "wildness."[11]

The themes most reported are those of chase or of destruction. According to Joseph Campbell, the "key issues" are those that propel us into the world of the unconscious, the world of the Familiar Self. The unconscious is the guiding force in each of our lives. (Those issues that take the attention of our unconscious minds are crucial to the process of human development. The issues are different for each of us, yet they must be faced with the knowledge that transformation to a higher spiritual understanding awaits the brave journeyer.) Ritual, myth, magical practices, and especially initiation are our guides into this realm.

When one does not understand how to address the unconscious directly through initiatory rites, then the initiatory images are provided spontaneously in dreams. When even this last avenue of communication is refused or ignored, dreams resort to images of fear in order to command the dreamer's attention. Images of passage become the images of horror—doom and eventual self disintegration.[12]

The knowledge of how to begin the healing process lies within the personal mythic realm of dreams and in initiation. There we must come to terms with the lost part of our soul.


# EXERCISE

Create a journal to record all of your dreams. What is the Familiar Self trying to say to you in your dreams? Which of the dream symbols do you feel has potential as an initiatory symbol?


# RITUAL

Draw a picture of one of your personal dream-initiatory images. Pay attention to color and shape choices. When you are done, take four white candles, place one at each corner of the drawing, and light them. Repeat the following affirmation three times:

> I ACCEPT THE SYMBOLS OF MY SPIRIT, FOR THEY SPEAK
> THE LANGUAGE OF MY FAMILIAR SELF. I ACCEPT THE
> PATH OF INITIATION TO WHICH THEY LEAD.

# EXERCISE:
# SELF-TEST FOR THE FAMILIAR SELF

Listed below are some questions to help you determine what animal you should anticipate meeting in your initiatory hunt during the Sacred Hunt meditation that follows.

Take some time to quietly contemplate each of the questions. Answer them honestly.

1. Do you prefer your "fun time" or "alone time" to be during the day or night?

2. Do you prefer day or nighttime hours for work?

3. Do you prefer the assurance of a regular dwelling place or the freedom to move at any time?

4. Do you feel most comfortable and natural maintaining a lifetime mate, or do you prefer to experience a series of relations?

5. What varieties of food do you naturally enjoy most (meats, grains, vegetables, etc.)?

6. Do you enjoy confrontation and competition, or you do avoid them?

7. Do your prefer to socialize in groups or would people consider you a loner?

8. In several adjectives (such as slow, angular, smooth, staccato, etc.), describe your usual physical movements.

9. Ask someone else to describe your physical movements in several adjectives.

10. Take a good look in the mirror with this question in mind: what animal do I look like?

11. If you could be any animal, which would it be? Why?

# EXAMINING YOUR ANSWERS

Each of the questions is designed to help you understand more about your personal animal behavior. This behavior might lend some insight to the Familiar Self within you. Some animals are group-oriented, some are loners; some mate for life and some don't, etc. Look at each of your answers and perhaps compare them to the various behaviors found in an animal encyclopedia. This may give you an idea of what Familiar Self you may expect to discover in the next exercise. Or, you can wait and be surprised!

# MEDITATION: THE SACRED HUNT

In the following meditation, you will discover your Familiar Self and will use all of your spirit senses to experience it. Try to remain open to the possibilities—the animal lying in wait may not be what you expected at all. In some cases, people have been greatly surprised to see an unexpected creature appear to them in the Sacred Hunt meditation. Sometimes it is a beast that repulses them! Still others seem to have sensed the animal of their Familiar Self long ago, so that the exercise only confirms their intuition.

Follow the instructions for relaxation as outlined in the Beginning Exercise of chapter 1. Once you are fully relaxed, turn on your tape recorder with the meditation below prerecorded, or have your partner begin reading.

**Reader:** You begin to float as a blue mist swirls about your body. As the swirling blue mist becomes a globe around you, you are lifted higher and higher. It takes you into the dream realm where you will begin your sacred journey.

(**Reader** pause for a moment)

Allow the blue globe of mist to disperse into the sunlit sky. See before you a lush, verdant forest, shrouded in mist. Many leafy trees stand closely together. In front of you, partially covered by ferns, there lies a path of rich, red earth leading into the darkened greenery beyond. From the depths of the forest, behind a large fern, a small child timidly peers out at the world. When it sees you, it runs back into the forest.

You follow the child and begin along the path that heads deep into the forest. The child running ahead of you is always just out of sight, disappearing here and there, under leafy ferns and shrubs. The deeper you venture into this enchanted realm, the deeper you relax. The deeper you relax, the more you create ties with the natural life force.

Soon the forest has become completely silent, except for one sound. It sounds like some kind of animal cry or just some rustling of leaves. Stop on the path for a moment. Listen and remember ... this is the sound of your animal power.

Follow the child now into a very dark grove of trees. The deeper you venture into the thicket, the more you relax and become one with the natural life force. Even though it is the middle of the day, here in the grove the Sun is virtually blotted out. It is very dark now. You can see neither the path before you, nor your hands or feet. Stop on the path for a moment. Hold your hands outstretched. You will feel your animal spirit guide brush up against your hands. Feel the texture of its body. Is it furry? Is it smooth? As soon as the animal came to you, it disappeared. But you will remember—for this is the touch of your animal power.

The child now takes you by the hand and leads you out of the darkness of the thicket and into the sunlight. You are led to the base of a great waterfall. Hear the roar of the waterfall as it tumbles into the pool below. You can smell the clean scent of the swirling misty air. But blending in with the smell of the water is the scent of an animal. What is the scent like? Remember it—this is the scent of your animal power.

From where you stand it is apparent that there is a path that leads behind the waterfall to a darkened cave. Blurred by the rushing water, you can see the vague, fleeting image of your child-guide darting into the cave. Follow the path behind the falls and enter the cave.

Once inside, the sounds of the falls are muffled. The cave walls feel warm and moist. The air does too. The cave seems darker as you go further into it. Darker and darker the cave becomes, until you cannot see anything. Call out to the child for help.

From the darkness, a glow appears, faintly at first. This light grows until it forms the outline or shadow of your animal power. It continues to glow brighter until the cave is fully illuminated and the animal likewise manifests itself fully. You can now see clearly your Familiar Spirit. Remember it. This is your animal of power.

Welcome it now and allow it to speak if it has any message for you.

(**Reader** pause for a moment.)

Know that you can return to this sacred cave at any time. This mystic place is the dwelling of the Familiar Self.

It is time to return to the physical world now. Allow the blue globe of mist to form and surround you now. It brings you back to your place of departure. You are returning now. You are here. When you feel ready, open your eyes.

Take a moment to recall your experience before answering the journaling questions.

# JOURNALING

What animal is your Familiar Self?

Describe in detail or draw the features of your animal power.

Is your Familiar Self male or female?

## THE FAMILIAR AS TEACHER

One of the powers of the Familiar Self is that of revealing mysteries and providing guidance, support, and teaching.[13] Many Native American myths reflect this. One in particular says:

> In the beginning of all things, wisdom and knowledge were with the animal. For Tirawa, the One Above, did not speak directly to man. He sent certain animals to tell mankind that he showed himself through the beast. And that from them, and from the stars and from the sun and the moon, man should learn.[14]

These beliefs are widespread among native North American peoples. The Tsistsistas of the plains have magical practitioners seek the animal powers to teach them all that they need to know.[15] In Australia, when people apprentice to shamans, they are taught that the Familiar assists the magical worker in the waking and dreaming states, and also acts as an informant.[16] In Siberia, shamans regularly hold conversations with their animal spirits[17] to deduce the nature of illnesses, to divine the future, and to give guidance to those in need. Finally, as Doreen Valiente and many other modern practitioners maintain, Familiar Spirits can be teachers for the Witch.[18]

Try the exercise below and then answer the questions in the section on Journaling. This exercise can be done whenever you need guidance or information about past, present, or future situations.

At the beginning of this exercise, you will again enter the cave in which you first met the Familiar Self. The image of the cave as an entrance into the meditation is a standard mythic form in the shamanic experiences of traditional magical workers. Entering the cave symbolizes the opening to the underworld of the shamans.

The Shaman . . . reaches an opening in the ground. The
most difficult stages of his adventure now begin, when the
depths of the underworld with their remarkable manifestations open before him. . . .[19]

The cave represents a crack through which the magical worker
slips into deeper parts of the psyche. It is also the womb opening of the
Great Earth Mother—patroness of the Witches. This is the cave where
you meet your Familiar Self when assistance or teachings are sought.

## EXERCISE: THE TEACHING FAMILIAR

Prior to your journey, think of a question that recently has been on
your mind. Take the question with you on this next trip to the cave.

Allow the blue globe of mist to take you again to that enchanted
forest, to the mouth of the cave where you met your Familiar Self. As
the blue mist dissipates into the surrounding atmosphere, see the cave
opening before you. You know the Familiar Self awaits you there, for
you can see the familiar glow emanating from the cave's depths.

Enter the cave and follow the light to the realm of the Familiar.

You see now your animal before you. Greet it and then ask it your
question. Wait now for an answer.

(**Reader** pause for a moment for the answer.)

Now that your question has been answered, it is time to return to
the outer realms. The blue mist envelops you and lifts you back to the
place of your departure.

## JOURNALING

Take a moment to recall the experience with the Familiar Self, the
question you asked and the answer you received.

What was your question?

What was your answer?

How did your Familiar Self communicate the answer (e.g., in words, in pictures, scratching in the dirt with its paw or talon)?

Was your answer clear and precise? Or was it mysterious and encoded?

What seems to be the personality of your Familiar Self?

Here are some potentially interesting questions you can pose to your Familiar Self: What is your name? How old are you? Where is it that you reside within me? What lessons or abilities do you have to teach me?

## NOTES

1. Russel Hope Robbins, *Encyclopedia of Witchcraft and Demonology* (New York: Crown Publishers, 1912), 190.

2. Evelyn Underhill, *Mysticism: A study in the nature and development of man's spiritual consciousness* (New York: E.P. Dutton and Co., 1911). See pt. 2, "The Mystic Way," chap. 2, "The Awakening Self."

3. Campbell, Joseph. *The Hero With a Thousand Faces* (New Jersey: Princeton University Press, 1973), 55.

4. Jeffrey Gantz, trans., *The Mabinogion* (London: Penguin Books, 1976), 46.

5. Patrick Ford, ed., *The Mabinogi and Other Medieval and Welsh Tales* (Berkeley: University of California Press, 1977), 37.

6. The fact that this is the first myth in the Mabinogi cycle establishes the importance of the sacred hunt and of meeting the Familiar Self.

7. Marie Antoinette Czaplicka, *Aboriginal Siberia* (London: Oxford University Press, 1969), 172, 179.

8. This is a state of heightened awareness during which individuals have sacred visions and can commune with the Gods. Ecstatic states are usually connected with shamanism.

9. Jon Christopher Crocker, *Vital Souls* (Tucson: University of Arizona Press, 1985), 292.

10. Campbell, 12.

11. Ann Faraday, *The Dream Game* (New York: Harper and Row, 1974), 241–5.

12. Campbell, 59–60.

13. Joseph Campbell and Bill Moyers, *The Power of Myth* (New York: Doubleday, 1988), 75.

14. Campbell and Moyers, 79.

15. Karl H. Schlesier, *The Wolves of Heaven* (Norman: University of Oklahoma Press, 1987), 12.

16. A.P. Elkin, *Aboriginal Men of High Degree* (St. Lucia, Queensland: University of Queensland Press, 1977), 13.

17. Czaplicka, 174; Vilmos Dioszegi and M. Hoppal, eds., *Shamanism in Siberia* (Budapest: Akadëmiai Kiadö, 1978), 42.

18. Doreen Valiente, *An ABC of Witchcraft* (New York: St. Martin's Press, 1973), 157.

19. Joseph Campbell, *The Hero* ... [cit.:] Harva, Uno, "Die religiösen Verstellungen der altaischen Völker." *Folklore Fellows Communications* 125, Helsinki 1938, 558–9.

# *the magical fetich*

Now in a cathedral, the imagery is in anthropomorphic form. God and Jesus and the saints and all are in human form. And in the caves the images are in animal form. But it's the same thing ... the form is secondary. The message is what is important.

— Joseph Campbell

Once initial contact with the Familiar Self has been established, it is time to begin creating the magical fetich.

The word "fetich" is the more archaic spelling of the word "fetish." I use it here to distinguish the potent magical tool from the sexual connotation this word has assumed over the last several decades. The fetich is an object used by a shaman to represent the powers of the Familiar Self. Though these objects can simply be found and then dedicated to magical work, ideally shamans create their fetiches themselves, imbuing them with the magical potency of the Familiar Self in the process.

Up until the Renaissance, Western culture always considered art an expression of the divine, and many Eastern cultures (Bali, for example) maintain this belief to this day. From earliest times, the

49

shaman has used the symbol language inherent in art as a means of tapping into the power of the animals.

Perhaps the earliest known magical art can be found in the caves of Trois Frères. There, painted on the huge cavern walls, is a representation of a half-man, half-animal dancer. He has an antlered head, round eyes, a long beard, animal paws for hands, and an animal's tail. He appears to be dancing (or at least in motion). Close by are other bison-men, similar in their hybrid human-animal form to the antlered dancer, also known as the "Sorcerer Les Trois Freres."[1] These images and the numerous ones like them seem to embody the transitional stage from the purely zoomorphic representations of Gods and Goddesses to the anthropomorphic forms.

As was suggested in the first chapter, the Gods of the European shamanic traditions were based on the earlier images of the Gods in animal form. As a matter of fact, Rodney Castleden, author of *The Stonehenge People,* states that it is more than likely that the tribal totem was used to represent the deity.[2] The animal-God/dess art motif found in ancient cultures is a well documented fact and is supported by a great body of archaeological evidence. Such evidence can be found in the recent excavations of the Neolithic community of Catal Huyuk in the Near East. James Mellaart, who headed those excavations, found a proliferation of animal-Goddess figurines.[3] Another authority on sacred art, Marija Gimbutas, explains in her work *Gods and Goddesses of Old Europe* that some 30,000 sculptures from over 300 archaeological excavation sites extending northward from the Aegean up through Czechoslovakia and the western Ukraine have been recovered, a good percentage of which are in the animal-God/dess form.[4] In her book, Gimbutas explores the Goddesses and Gods represented in largely animal forms; among the most common of these forms are the dog, doe, bear, turtle and toad, and bee and butterfly.[5]

Much of this early sacred art is thought to represent shamans at work. Cave paintings such as those of Trois Frères, and many of the animal figurines found all over Europe, are tied to a form of ritual called sympathetic magic. In this magic, images were created to represent the deity connected with a particular animal that may have been a food mainstay of a tribe. This was done as a form of petition to the deities prior to the hunt. The cave paintings are thought to represent

*The Sorcerer of Trois Frères*

cave painting, Lascaux, c. 15,000 BCE

shamans in the animal-God disguise. This too was done by the
shamans to insure a successful hunt.

The preponderance of sacred animal art found in the Upper Pale-
olithic and Neolithic excavations indicates that animals must have
been essential to the magical life of the tribe.

Today, use of the fetich and magical animal art is prevalent particularly in the native societies of North America, Africa, New
Guinea, and the West Indies.[6]

# WHY THE FETICH?

As discussed earlier, the Familiar Self communicates nonverbally; its
speech is encoded in the tactile, visual, auditory, olfactory, and even
gustatory faculties. Art is an activity that often coordinates several of
these physical senses, and this is particularly true of the act of creating
sacred art. In fact, any type of hands-on, creative activity will stir the
animal nature within. Entire dialogues can be conducted with the animal power solely through the senses, without the often inadequate
intermediary of language.

Once completed, the fetich should only be used in conjunction
with Familiar rituals and meditations of empowerment.[7]

# CONSTRUCTION

Constructing the fetich should be undertaken with air of ceremony,
yet also with a sense of ingenuity and fun. During the creative process
you want to allow your unconscious processes to take over. As you create, allow the conscious mind's tendency to judge and comment upon
your actions to fade away. The conscious mind may want to persuade
you that certain color choices or anatomical proportions are dubious,
but it is to your benefit to ignore such misgivings. The construction
period is the time to trust the inner animal self for inspiration.

Understand that the fetich is meant to reflect the landscape of the
soul. Therefore, one of the most important aspects to this work is to allow
the nonphysical aspects of the animal spirit to shine through the physical
artwork. In other words, let the fetich be a symbol of your spiritual power.

*Fetiches from Dahomey*

from *The History of Man* by J.W. Buel (Richmond, 1889)

The cave paintings in Trois Frères and the animal figurines studied by Mellaart and Gimbutas stand as illustrations of the fact that the primitive artists were hardly concerned with perspective, anatomy, or proportion—at least that which is understood or considered aesthetically pleasant to cowan[8] viewers. To the untrained eye the sacred imagery of the ancients may appear misshapen; the eyes, nose, mouth, or even the whole head may be missing; the sexual anatomy may be vague; or it may combine the body parts of many different species. But the meaning of this mythic imagery was not intended to be revealed to those of purely mundane consciousness.[9] They are not "misshapen" due to any technical inability. They are not supposed to be representations of a physical reality, but rather the unseen reality which is then given a physical form.[10] The visions of a magical worker are best understood when magical consciousness is assumed.

The fetich can be made of any substance or combination of pieces you want. Here is a list of materials common to fetich making:

| | | | |
|---|---|---|---|
| clay | beads | wax | fossils |
| mud | bones[11] | leaves | sand |
| sticks | crystals | teeth | live plants |
| twigs | semiprecious stones | coins | seashells |
| stones | hair | amulets | nuts |
| feathers | fur | herbs | scraps of metal |
| glass | small bells | seaweed | |

# BEFORE WORKING

To begin, take a moment to go into an altered state. Do the Beginning Exercise, go to the cave dwelling of the Familiar Self and ask it what materials might be used in the construction. Some familiars may suggest or show materials readily available around the house. Others may guide you to materials that may require some searching on your part.

# JOURNALING

Use the space below to design your fetich. How would it look?

What materials would you use?

What symbols of power would you inscribe on the fetich (for example, spirals, paw prints, lightning rods, flowers, etc.)? Sketch these here.

# CLEANSING AND BLESSING

Gather the materials and hold a small cleansing ritual for them.

## WHAT YOU'LL NEED

- The materials for crafting your fetich
- The four elements:

  A dish of earth
  A bowl of water
  A red candle
  Lit incense

Envision charging each of the elements with your personal power. Then take each of the crafting materials and pass them through each of the elements, saying:

> I CLEANSE THEE WITH THE ELEMENT OF (AIR, FIRE, WATER, OR EARTH).

Because this is a symbolic gesture of consecration, you need only sprinkle each of the materials with Earth and Water; pass them through the heat of the candle flame to charge with Fire and through the incense smoke for Air. Once you have completed this for all materials, ask the Familiar Self, once again, what the design of the fetich should be. The design may come to you visually. It may come through words, or you may just know how it is supposed to be. Not everyone will perceive their design in the same way. Remain patient and open to all possibilities.

# DRAWING DOWN THE FAMILIAR

After your fetich is created, you need to draw into it your Familiar powers. Here is a ceremony for drawing down the Familiar. "Drawing Down the Moon" is a traditional Wiccan rite in which the Goddess is drawn into the body of an attending priestess. Just as we would draw the Goddess down into the priestess, so here are we drawing the Familiar Self power into the fetich.

## WHAT YOU'LL NEED

- Your finished fetich
- A small bowl of salt
- A small bowl of water
- A red candle
- Totem Spirit incense[12]
- Totem Spirit oil
- Four votive candles
- A piece of parchment at least 8" x 8"
- A red-inked pen

In this ritual, you will dedicate your completed fetich to the Universal Powers and imbue it with the life of the Familiar.

Place three scoops of the salt (which represents Earth in this ritual) into the bowl of water and stir. Take a few drops of the saltwater mixture and anoint the figurine, saying:

I IMBUE THEE WITH THE ELEMENTS OF THE GODDESS.

Next, light the Totem Spirit incense and pass the fetich through the smoke. Light the red candle and briefly hold it over the open flame, saying:

I IMBUE THEE WITH THE ELEMENTS OF THE GOD.

Anoint the fetich with Totem Spirit oil, smearing some on the top and bottom of the artwork. Using the same oil, anoint your own brow. Touch the fetich to your own third eye (on your brow between your eyes) to create a psychic link. Hold the figurine up high and say:

THOU ART NO LONGER OF CLAY AND WAX,
OF BONE OR BEAD, OF TWIG OR FLAX.
FROM THIS TIME FORTH THINE EVERY PART
SHALL BE AN INSTRUMENT OF MY ART!

Breathe onto the fetich three times, exerting your magical will and visualizing light entering the figure with each exhalation. Continue by saying:

BECOME NOW A WORTHY VESSEL FOR MY FAMILIAR POWERS.

Hold the figure between your palms and envision your Familiar Self entering the fetich, giving it life.

With the red-inked pen, draw a circle on the parchment paper. Use your imagination to see the circle as a container of your magical power. Place the fetich inside the circle and light the four votive candles, one placed at each compass direction on the perimeter of the drawn circle.

Allow the fetich energies to settle undisturbed, until the candles are completely burned out. Now your fetich is ready for magical work.

## NOTES

1. Marija Gimbutas, *The Language of the Goddess* (San Francisco: Harper-Collins, 1989), 175.

2. Rodney Castleden, *The Stonehenge People: An Exploration of Life in Neolithic Britain 4700-2000 B.C.* (London: Routledge Kegan Paul, 1987), 228.

3. See, for example, James Mellaart, *Catal Hüyük* (New York: McGraw Hill, 1967), 24.

4. See, for example, Marija Gimbutas, *Gods and Goddesses of Old Europe* (London: Thames and Hudson, Ltd., 1974).

6. Castleden, 228.

7. Marija Gimbutas, *Gods and Goddesses of Old Europe*, 169–191. Turtle and toad are listed together since they both represent the Goddess as a human fetus. Bee and butterfly are listed together because both are thought to represent the Goddess of transformation.

8. Cowan means "uninitiated" in Wiccan terminology.

9. Gimbutas, *Gods and Goddesses of Old Europe*, 38.

10. Ibid.

11. One interesting idea about the use of bones is that some of the ancients believed that bones were the dwelling place of the animal soul after death. Incorporating bones into the fetich was an effort to use the soul of the animal as an aid to magical workings.

12. Gimbutas, *Gods and Goddesses of Old Europe*, 38.

# SECTION 2

## *transformation*

# *paths to transformation*

## THE CHARGE OF DIONYSUS:

*Come to me, children of change,*
*For I am thy Lord; I am Dionysus of the Thracian glade.*
*Born am I of human womb. Born am I as well from the thigh*
*Of mighty Zeus. Know now the mystery: God and Man am I.*
*At the gates of transformation I await thee,*
*Ecstasy is thine only key.*
*Where bud finds its blossom, there am I.*
*Where tadpole transfigures to toad, there am I.*
*Where darkness drowns in light, there am I.*
*Where Woman becomes Goddess and Man becomes God,*
*There am I too.*
*For I dwell in the place of rhythm within all,*
*I dance to the beat of thy passion and yearning for change.*

ne of the basic tools of animal magic is knowledge. The more techniques one knows for raising spiritual energy and using it along with the Familiar Self to change consciousness, the more one's growth and personal power increase. Greater attention to consciously raising these states will be the focus of the advanced Familiar workings that follow.

There are many techniques conducive to these enhanced states of consciousness. One of these you have already explored: meditation. Other well-known and effective techniques used by shamans and Witches include drumming and "trance-dancing." There are many other paths as well. However, the end result of these practices is the same: a state of ecstasy.

What exactly is ecstasy?

In the magical lexicon, "ecstasy" refers to a temporary state of greatly increased internal and, ultimately, external awareness. Magical ecstasy is the primary path through which the Witch, no matter what his or her cultural background, obtains power. Ecstatic experiences are often called "trance states."[1] This trance state has been said to come in two varieties. The first comes through an out-of-body experience; the second comes through an inner journeying state.[2] The latter kind is of interest to the Familiar magical worker.

To the Witch and initiate of the mysteries, ecstasy represents a journey to the very brink of the Goddess and God realm. Once at this brink, the Witch is able to commune directly with Deity and all of its manifestations, be they mineral, plant, or animal, physical or non-physical, known or unknown. At this point, the ecstatic internalizes these powers and ignites the Divine within.

The mythology of the "twice born" Dionysus, the ancient Greek God of ecstasy, provides clues to the spiritual potential for all who engage in ecstatic practices. The myths centering around his life tell that he was a child both human and divine.

Myths, of course, act much like a cosmic mirror reflecting the human soul in its potential perfection. In light of this, we might say that Dionysus' story conveys the message that each of us has the potential to become perfect incarnations of humanity and divinity when we enter the realm of ecstasy. As Nietzsche said, the "Dionysiac condition" tends "toward the shattering of the individual and his fusion with the original Oneness."[3]

During a conference led by anthropologist Michael Harner, founder of the Foundation for Shamanic Studies, a discussion arose centering around the practice of herbal induction of ecstasy. Harner reported that long before the use of herbal substances for inducing

*A Traditional Form of Trance-Dancing—Whirling Dervishes*

from *The Occult Review* XV.5, May 1912

ecstasy, the primary vehicle for this among certain traditional, magical peoples (including the European Witches) was drumming. In areas of Siberia, church authorities who wanted to stamp out pagan magical practices brought charges against anyone found with a drum.[4]

The Siberian shamans discovered herbal substitutes[5] for the drum that would quietly and effectively induce ecstasy through intoxication. True, the shaman was able to create the state of ecstasy without the use of the drum, but the price was often extreme illness and even death.

Throughout the European Renaissance, the voluminous trial records documenting the confessions of alleged Witches contain many stories that refer to the use of "ointments." Many of these are strikingly similar in content and use to those of the Siberian shamans; the hallucinogenic effects were always the same. Various accounts of changing into animals,[6] magical flights, meetings in the woods during blizzards, and other seemingly impossible feats were just a few of the commonly reported experiences.

That these divergent magical peoples reported transforming into animals is an important clue to the inner workings of Familiar magic. Through ecstatic practices, they were able to set aside the conscious mind and thereby throw open the realm of the unconscious to such a degree that "transformation" occurred.

# EXERCISE

Take a moment to recall the physical sensations you felt immediately following your inner journeys in the previous meditations. The light, centered, or slightly "buzzed" feelings are the residual effects of mild ecstasy.

In the next sections of the book you will explore the transformative and ecstasy-inducing powers of dancing and drumming. These arts, once learned, will be the springboard for later exercises and experiences.

## NOTES

1. Vilmos Dioszegi and M. Hoppal, eds., *Shamanism in Siberia* (Budapest: Akadïmiai Kiadö, 1978), 41.

2. Dioszegi and Vilmos, 42.

3. Bernard F. Dukore, *Dramatic Theory and Criticism* (San Francisco: Duke Reinhart and Winston Inc., 1974), 823. Excerpted from *The Birth of Tragedy and The Genealogy of Morals* by Friedrich Nietzsche.

4. Paraphrasing from lecture series held at the Esalen Institute, Big Sur, California, January 1990.

5. Michael J. Harner, *Hallucinogens and Shamanism* (New York: Oxford University Press, 1973), xii. Harner lists a mushroom called fly-agaric as the main ingredient. Allegedly this mushroom produces hallucinogenic effects and "light forms of intoxication." I would not use this, nor would I recommend its use. This is a highly toxic fungus.

6. From the body of knowledge surrounding the modern craft, it is commonly believed that the high priest or male leader of a coven would often dress in the skins of an antlered or horned animal. The high priest, dressed as such, represented the God of the hunt and was symbolic of the stag who loses his horns in an annual cycle of death and rebirth.

   Harner suggests that tactile surroundings greatly affect the experience of someone under the narcotic influence of an "ointment." Traditional Wiccan religious costuming, combined with the effects of this ointment, leaves little doubt as to the reason for the innumerable accounts of Witches who claimed they had changed into animals or had seen someone transform. See Harner, 141.

# *drumming*

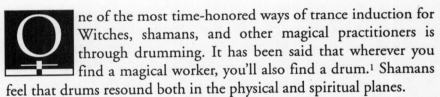ne of the most time-honored ways of trance induction for Witches, shamans, and other magical practitioners is through drumming. It has been said that wherever you find a magical worker, you'll also find a drum.[1] Shamans feel that drums resound both in the physical and spiritual planes.

Since the big bang of creation, which could be considered the first of all drumbeats, everything else in the universe has grown from its reverberation, as Mickey Hart said in his book *Drumming on the Edge of Magic,* forming the galaxies, solar systems, the planets, and us.[2]

Even the most basic physics text will tell you that all matter is pulsating vibration. Subatomic particles pulsate to create atoms, which in turn pulsate to create molecules, which in turn pulsate in combinations, creating the varied forms of matter. From our recent understandings of physics, we know that apparently solid matter is actually 96 percent empty space. What gives us the impression of solidity is the way this space vibrates.

The magical worker's job is to synchronize with these vibrations which permeate matter and spirit.

Drumming is the traditional magical way of tuning into and actually vibrating at the same rate as other objects. At the same time, the drumbeat opens the psyche, promoting a sustained Familiar-self consciousness.

The modern, "scientifically approved" shamans (at least the ones we call psychologists) have understood that the metronomic effects of a steady drumbeat can take the listener into deep levels of consciousness[3] and have measured the hypnotic effects of the metronomic beat from at least as early as 1902.

Our technical understanding of the effects of metronomic beats may be clinically defined, dissected, and understood in the lab. But drumming has clearly been understood and used as one of the tools of traditional magical folk from well before recorded history.[4] Drumming (or its metronomic equivalent) lulls the conscious mind into abeyance, thereby inducing trance or an ecstatic state. The hypnotic effects of the incessant beat are useful for attaining deeper levels of consciousness,[5] from where the shaman can call forth the Familiar spirits.

Most of the recorded native ceremonies throughout the world show the drum's centrality to the spiritual life of the community. In these cultures, drums and other percussive instruments act as bridges between the realms of the humans, animals, and Gods: "The drum itself . . . becomes the very axis of power that reveals the Universe to an otherwise isolated individual [namely, the shaman]."[6]

It is said that magical drummers are very close to nature and as such they recognize the value of the life force which manifests in the physical form of animals, who give birth to the components of the drum.[7] It is therefore not unusual for some sort of homage to be paid to the animal spirit for its life energies that are given to manifest in literally different vibrations.[8] This is quite similar to the theme of life springing forth from death, which has been one of the basic mythic motifs of many of the high civilizations throughout time.

Traditional cultures consider the drum to have many powers. For instance, it transports the shaman into the spirit dimension, or lends power in evoking various spirits (including Familiars) by its sounds.[9] In Japan, native magical workers use drums to call up the spirits of the deities,[10] who usually become manifest in their ancestral, totemic, animal form.

*Gypsy Drum and Other Instruments*
from *The History of Man* by J.W. Buel (Richmond, 1889)

# THE RHYTHMS OF MAGIC

Drums necessarily imply rhythm and rhythm is an important part of magical life. Rhythm is acknowledged both in its symbolic and literal forms within the context of magic and transformation.

Rhythms pervade the universe in what is called the macrocosm, or "the big picture." This is illustrated in such events as the big bang, or even the circling of planets around star-suns.

Rhythms are also reflected on our planet and in our personal lives, in what is called the microcosm.

The rhythm of life begins with birth; the next beat of the drum is growth, or youth. Next comes mid-life and the next is death. But death is but the beginning of yet deeper, more resonant rhythms. Our seasons occur in rhythms guided by the rhythm of the Sun: Fall, Winter, Spring, and Summer.

The Moon dances in the heavens, reflecting the light of the Sun. Since the Moon is reflective and cyclical, it is properly female in its symbolic manifestation.

The Moon shows her face as first the Maiden of the waxing, young crescent Moon, then the Mother of the Full Moon, then the old wise

Crone of the waning and dark Moon. Other rhythms include North, South, East, and West. Hot, cold. Day, night. Year in, year out. And the beat unendingly continues.

It is encoded within our very being to be rhythmic. The drumbeat specifically and rhythm in general are the very territory of the magical Familiar Self. To be sure, the old adage that "music soothes the savage beast" has its validity and applies to our Familiar Selves. But let us elaborate on this adage and add to it that music—more specifically one of its component parts, the drumbeat—can also excite the beast, as well as anger it or elate it.

# EXERCISES

The proper starting place lies in practicing basic drumbeats at first. Once the basics have been mastered, you will move into the more advanced work of creating magical rhythm in chapter 8.

# THE FOUR-BEAT

As we noted earlier, the number four relates to the ever-changing seasons. Four also corresponds to the compass directions and to the alchemical elements of Air, Fire, Water, and Earth. So our first natural beat is in four.

The four-beat can be broken down into a series of single beats. The number one represents and contacts the masculine energy within. Drumming the four-beat balances any lack or excess of this energy. Male energy is active and penetrating in our polar paradigm of the God and Goddess. Think of the four-beat as it is used in marches and usually straightforward dances, again emphasizing its active and penetrating nature. Dances that are performed to the three-beat, which we will explore later, are traditionally done in circles and spirals (for instance, the waltz).

As you work with the four-beat, scan your body for any signs of tension or fatigue. Are you are beating very loudly on the drum, or is your beater (if you have one) being held in a death-grip? These signs of tension are psychic evidence of either a lack or excess of male energy.

The outward symptoms of lack of male energy include constant fatigue, laziness, diabetes, hypoglycemia, impotence, low vitality, lack of drive or ambition, indecision, and weight gain. Too much male energy can cause tension, headaches, hypersexuality, aggression, hostility, hypertension, and ulcers.[11] Use the four-beat to balance either the lack or an excess of male energy. Use the four-beat to contact male-energy oriented animals.

## SOME DRUMMING TIPS

Here are some tips for beginning drummers:

To assist you in keeping a steady beat, try saying the word "and" between beats as you drum:

1 and 2 and 3 and 4 and 1 and 2 and 3 and 4 . . . etc.

You should strike the drumhead on each of the numbers one through four and pause for a silent beat on each "and." Practice often, because the more you work with basic rhythm, the less you'll need to depend on the mechanics of saying "and" between numbers in order to maintain an even beat.

There are an infinite number of variations on the basic four-beat. For instance you can have:

1 and 2 and 3 (and 4 — silent) and 1 and 2 (and 3 and 4) . . . repeat.

The number one is always emphasized in the basic four-beat. You might also try double beats on some of the numbers, while others continue to remain single beats. You can combine any amount of double beats, single beats, and pauses to create the rhythm you like within the format of the four-beat.

## THE THREE-BEAT

The three-beat is the same beat as "waltz time." In music notation it is also known as 3/4 time. Three has been a potently magical number since magical systems arose. When music was first notated, it was always counted in three time, because that pattern was thought to be the rhythm of the divine principle. As late as the Middle Ages, Christianity considered any song heretical if it was written outside of the three-beat.

Since magic is linked to one of our principle luminaries, the Moon, the female principle of manifestation, plenty of "three symbolism" arises. The Moon wanes and waxes in three magical phases. These phases herald the beginning and ending of specific cycles of energies: waxing Moon—the time of beginnings; Full Moon—the time of fertility and fruition; and the waning Moon—time of decay and return. The three phases of the feminine principle correlate with these Moon phases as well: the Maiden of potential, the Mother of completion, and the Crone of wisdom.

In ancient agricultural societies, the earliest breakdown of the seasonal year was in three. The seasons consisted of Spring, Summer, and a combination of Fall and Winter: birth, growth, and return, or death. The number three was adopted by Western theology and manifested in the Christian's "Holy Trinity." This trinity was supposedly "three Gods in one": a father God, His son, and a "Holy Spirit." Ironically, the number three is typically associated with Goddess energy, yet the feminine in the Christian trinity of godhead has been completely eradicated.

Three is an important beat in re-establishing this lost balance with feminine energies. The female energies are the polar opposite to the male energies and are the necessary, complementary forces with which to make magic. Feminine energies are receptive in our paradigm of God and Goddess, which correspond to manifestation and the Earth realm.

An internal imbalance of feminine energy can cause fatigue or tension during the three-beat drumming. Watch for it as you experiment. Lack of feminine energy in the physical plane causes density of mind, harshness, coldness, an uncaring attitude, frigidity, stinginess, and secretiveness. An excess can cause disorientation, inability to focus, physical lightheadedness, bladder or kidney problems.[12] If you notice any symptoms of lack or excess, use the three-beat to help balance this.

## WHAT KINDS OF DRUMS TO USE

What type of drum is the best for work with the Familiar? Whatever kind speaks to you. You may not even like the sound of drums, or you may be sensitive to loud noises. In these cases, you may want to try a

*Waganda Drums*
from *The History of Man* by J.W. Buel (Richmond, 1889)

tambourine, rattles, or clacking sticks. Go to a good music store and try out different percussion instruments on your own. Listen to each instrument and let its vibration ring through you. If you hit the right one, the Familiar Self will answer back. You will know intuitively which instrument is best for you.

Many students want to equip themselves with the proper tools of the magical trade. At the same time, they might be reluctant to spend pots of money on expensive ritual equipment. This is especially the case when a student is just starting out and experimenting with the magical path. After all, magic, Wicca, and other forms of shamanic practice are not for everyone and no one wants to get stuck with a bunch of stuff they won't ever use.

My suggestion for an inexpensive and durable drum is the Remo pre-tuned hand drum. This was the first drum I bought for myself, and I still lend it out to students today. The Remo comes in many sizes, ranging in price from about $15 to $400. I like Remo drums because of their weatherproof heads. When doing work outdoors, the heat, humidity, or cold can adversely effect a standard animal-skin-headed drum. Besides this, the weatherproof head can be painted with leather paints, and magical sigils on your drum can be both spiritually beneficial and aesthetically pleasing.

# JOURNALING

What internal differences do you detect in the three-beat and the four-beat?

Make a list of the beats to which you are more naturally aligned. What energy differences did you detect within yourself while you engaged in three and four beats?

Note too any corresponding emotional states (examples: the four-beat seems useful when I am angry; the three-beat makes me feel playful; etc.).

What have been the rhythms of my life up to now?

What rhythms do I see in the lives of others?

What happens when I try to ignore or go against a natural rhythm in my life?

# EXERCISE: THE FAMILIAR RHYTHM

Once you obtain a drum or other percussion instrument, use the guided imagery in chapter 4 to take you once again to the cave dwelling of your Familiar Self. Ask your Familiar Self what rhythm will call its presence forth.

When you know this, you can summon your Familiar Self whenever you need its assistance through the power of the drum.

# NOTES

1. Marie Antoinette Czaplicka, *Aboriginal Siberia* (London: Oxford University Press, 1969), 203.

2. Mickey Hart, *Drumming at the Edge of Magic* (New York: HarperCollins Publishers, 1990), 11.

3. Alvin C. Halphide, *Mind and Body* (Chicago: Monarch Book Company, 1899), 62.

4. John A. Grim, *The Shaman: Patterns of Siberian and Ojibway Healing* (Norman: University of Oklahoma Press, 1983).

5. Grim, 159.

6. Grim, 78–9.

7. Alan P. Merriam, *The Anthropology of Music* (Chicago: Northwestern University Press, 1964), 77.

8. Dioszegi and Vilmos, *Tracing Shamans in Siberia,* 62.

9. Czaplicka, 203.

10. Michael Czaja, *Gods of Myth and Stone* (New York: Weatherhill, 1974), 190.

11. See, for example, Anodea Judith, *Wheels of Life: A Users Guide to the Chakra System* (St. Paul, Minnesota: Llewellyn Publications, 1988).

12. See, for example, Judith, *Wheels of Life.*

# dance and the art of shapeshifting

Some saie they can transubstantiate themselves and others,
and take the forms and shapes of asses, wolves, ferrets, cows,
apes, horses, etc.

—Reginold Scot, 1584[1]

## EARTH DANCES

The most universal form of human communication is movement. Gestural expression has the ability to transcend formal language barriers. No doubt early folk used the human body as a means of communication with the mysterious forces of nature and the invisible world of spirits around them. Through ritualized movement and specialized dances of power, our ancestors entered the realm of the ecstatic and, therefore, the Familiar.

For hunting societies, ecstatic dance was a way of summoning the totem and its power.[2] Animal dances were one of the most essential ingredients in the workings of primitive magic; they were used to tap into the very pulse of nature.

Traditional magical practitioners usually created their power dances to mimic the movements of the animals around them. When the shaman dressed in the hide of the totem animal and behaved as it did, there was no distinction between the shaman and the Animal-God—between "the dancer and the dance," as Yeats expressed it.

Some of the earliest recorded dances connecting the Witches to their shamanic ancestors were fertility circle-dances. In Great Britain these were most popular during Spring's elaborate May Day celebrations.[3] At that time the religious leaders, the villagers, and country folk would perform ring-dances around the phallic Maypole as a celebration of the life-force in nature.[4] Ring-dancing became so popular in pagan Northern Europe that in 589 CE the Church, as part of its campaign to eradicate heathen practices, decreed a formal ban on dancing. To this day, some Christian sects frown upon dancing on Sunday.

Many of these folk dances have been passed from generation to generation as part of the shamanic legacy of the modern magical traditions, such as Wicca. However, the Witch is only one of many magical practitioners who use dance in ritual. The Zuni of New Mexico do specialized deer dances at certain times of the year to invoke the aid of these woodland creatures.[5] The shamans of the Yakut district of Siberia dance in animal skins in order to summon the power of their familiars.[6] The buffalo dance is still enacted by the Native Americans, specifically by members of the Blackfoot tribe. And in Northern Europe (in Abbott's Bromley, England) the horn dance[7] is still performed by men who dress in the skins and antlers of elk—a remnant of the animal dances performed by Witches centuries ago.

Little has changed over the centuries in the practice of magical dance; it has remained a potent path for even the most seasoned magical adept. Today, many different earth religions and magical folk continue to use dance to free their wild, spontaneous, instinctive animal selves.

## FIRST STEPS IN VISION DANCING

The experience of magical energy that passes from the Familiar to the human world is best generated through what native magical people call "vision dances." Such a dance is designed to induce an ecstatic

*The Emu Dance of Australia*
from *The History of Man* by J.W. Buel (Richmond, 1889)

state, during which the dancer experiences visions through the animal power. Native American writer Jamake Highwater says that most Westerners have a hard time separating the experience of dance from its associations with "mindless amusement."[8] Perhaps this is because Western society tends to support and emphasize communication through the mode of language, but not especially through gesture. When one is acculturated to believe that self-expression is best achieved through words, the potential for using the entire body is diminished. However, the physical body and the spirit are inextricably linked. As Highwater later points out, Native Americans have always been in touch with this; for them, dancing is the breath of life made visible.[9] Through dance, the magical expression of "as above, so below" is powerfully exemplified. Our bodies are the sacred dwelling places of the Gods and of our Familiar Selves. When we dance we not only celebrate this indwelling of spirit, but we move it and energize it.

The following exercises will be beneficial in developing the skills needed for the shapeshifting exercise. Below are some guidelines for effective vision dancing:

## WARM UP

Be sure to limber up the body with some gentle stretching before you do any physical movement—especially trance-dance. Once deep in trance, many people exert themselves beyond their usual capabilities; it can be easy to ignore a pulled muscle in the process.

## DANCE WITH YOUR EYES HALF-CLOSED

This limits your mundane visual perception, allowing inner vision to come to the fore. Nevertheless, dancing with your eyes partially open is important for insuring your physical safety, even if you are dancing in an open, flat space. The conscious mind will not relinquish its innate defenses without some measure of security in reference to the surrounding terrain.

## ALLOW YOUR EXPRESSION TO BE SPONTANEOUS

Carl Jung said in *The Spirit of Art, Man and Literature*[10] that "nothing is more injurious to immediate experience than cognition." Try releasing your sense of "cognition" during the exercise and allow the experience of the dance to take over. Do not make any concerted effort to keep on the beat. Rhythmic prowess is neither the point nor a concern of the exercise. Not only that, but it would be surprising for someone completely given over to Familiar consciousness to remain on beat. A good way to tell if someone has not completely let go of the ego and submerged into Familiar consciousness is if they remain on beat throughout the whole of the dance exercise.

When we depart from the formal, structured rhythms and connect with the inner ones, we become much more spontaneous and free. We then begin to dance in the cosmic round; we join in the ancient circle dance of the Witch.

# EXERCISE: VISION DANCE

## ITEMS NEEDED

- A drumming tape or a partner to do the drumming.

- A private, empty space large enough to accommodate free movement, or any secluded spot in nature such as a wooded glade, an open field, a beach, or a park.

## BEGINNING THE DANCE

Begin the dance standing in the center of a circle you mark with eight stones or votive candles.

Have your partner begin drumming or turn on your tape. Keep your eyes half closed. Listen to the music, let the rhythms sweep over your being, and begin to connect with the movements of your inner self.

Allow the rhythms to suggest (not define) your movements. Is the beat sharp or soft? Is it quick or slow? See what your body's inner response is and let the dance become as wild or as tame as your internal rhythm dictates. Let your Familiar Self suffuse your being; allow it to run and become powerful again.

## VARIATION DANCE EXERCISE

This is a sitting variation on the previous exercise, and is intended for those who have limited space in which to work.

In this exercise, you can allow your eyes to fully close. Sit crosslegged on the floor. As the drumming begins, allow the chest, arms, and all upper body parts to move freely to the pulsating rhythms. From this sitting position, you can generate the rest of your dance.

## YET ANOTHER VARIATION

If you have found several magical partners with whom to practice, get them all together and have each one try trance dancing blindfolded. This requires not only someone to drum, but others who should act as spotters, watching the dancer. The spotters must stay near enough to the dancer to keep her or him from harm's way. The spotters should also be there to lend energy to the dance.

One final note: Each time you trance-dance, the style, intensity, and mood of the experience will change. It will never be the same from one session to the next. Count on it. Dance and ecstasy are experiences of the moment. Focusing within the mental framing of "the immediate" and "the now" can be a whole new experience in itself for some.

# JOURNALING

How does my body respond to different kinds of drumbeats?

What can I do to improve my ability to vision dance?

*The Frog Dance of Australia*
from *The History of Man* by J.W. Buel (Richmond, 1889)

# SHAPESHIFTING

Shapeshifting is the art of transforming in consciousness from the purely human to the purely Familiar. Magical transformation into the animal self is a practice that has been long observed by tribal societies and is a magical remnant of the hunting rites performed thousands of years ago by the first shamans.[11]

Taliesin, the 6th-century Celtic bard and shaman,[12] wrote in the *Cad Goddeu* about his many shapeshifting experiences:

> I was in many shapes. . . .
> I was an eagle. . . .
> I was a snake on an enchanted hill.
> I was a viper in a lake. . . . [13]

In other writings, Taliesin assumes the forms of a buck, bull, cat, cockerel, dog, fox, goat, hare, marten, roebuck, salmon, sow, squirrel, stallion, wolf, crane, and eagle.[14]

Shapeshifting remained a popular theme of magical lore and rite in Northern Europe long after the Christian calendar was recognized. These rites were enactments of the covenant that tribal people held with the animal world. The shaman would attempt to contact the animal to be hunted by dressing in the skins of that animal, acting out its movements and sounds. Through this the shaman would transform into the animal and then journey with its spirit to the realm of the Goddess[15] to petition for a successful hunt.

With the later shift in emphasis from hunting to agriculture, the Goddess (as Earth Mother and provider of grain) supplanted the animal spirits. Gradually, the act of magical transformation became less associated with physical survival and more linked with healing and spiritual needs. The ritual act of transformation became a way for the shaman to attune more deeply with nature, to be shown power and to commune with cosmic life.[16]

Shapeshifting was a popular theme in the Northern European myths, especially Celtic ones. For instance, in the story of Math, son of Mathonwy, the principal character, a powerful sorcerer, turns his nephews Gwidion and Gilfaethwy into a hind and a stag for a year, a pig and sow for the following year, and then a wolf and bitch in the third year. He says to them: "Let your nature be the same as that of the animals in whose shape you are."[17] Thus did Math teach them about their animal natures. As the story continues, each year the transformed pair would come to Math with their offspring whom he would confiscate and change into human children. Here, once again, is there an illustration of transformation—only in reverse. The shapeshifting of each child is reminiscent of what was earlier observed: the Familiar Self links to the "child within."

Once the Church began to exert real authority in the Western world, religious censorship began in earnest, yet threats made by the Church initially did little to stop the practice of shapeshifting. Throughout the Middle Ages and into the late 1600s in Europe, and in colonial America as late as the 1700s, the belief persisted that Witches could "assume what bodies they please, and appear in any figure or shape."[18]

# THE MODERN WITCH AND TRANSFORMATION

Shapeshifting is one of the magical inheritances of the wild Witch. With this heritage comes tremendous power. Of course, the transformation for which students of the Craft strive is purely a psychic one. The main goal of magic, once again, is to be able to change consciousness at will. Through the act of shapeshifting, you empower the Familiar Self; and when the Familiar Self has been empowered, it can effect far-ranging, dramatic changes on the levels of healing, knowledge, intuition, and spiritual connection.

# TECHNIQUES TO BE USED

One of the most widely used inductions into the transformative state, as practiced by shamans of Northern Europe, Siberia, and South America, is the dance of imitation.[19] Through imitative dances, the Familiar Self is evoked in its most potent and uninhibited form.

Imitative dances are the very key to displacement of the conscious mind and its processes, which set the bounds of ordinary reality. These dances return us to those primal stages of human infancy when the unconscious mind was unfettered. This realm of the unconscious, the wilderness of the Familiar, is the misty forest clearing in which we strive to meet in order to dance and to orchestrate the whole of the cosmos.

Once the Familiar is evoked, its power takes over and the magical worker transforms. He or she then assumes the full powers of the Familiar. The magical worker is at once in control and controlled. The control is not specifically that of the Familiar itself; rather it acts as the vehicle for Universal Power.

# EXERCISE: TRANSFORMATION

Just as you did in the first ecstatic dance and drumming exercises, you need to relax into the experience of transformation. This is a powerful experience, and requires the preliminary steps of ecstatic dance to be truly effective. Be sure to work with those exercises enough that you become comfortable with them. Surrendering complete control might feel risky at first, but it soon becomes a powerfully liberating experience.

In order to transform successfully, you will need either a partner to drum for you or a drumming tape. If you make your own drumming tape, be sure it lasts at least 10–15 minutes. Being midway through transformation when the drumming stops can be disorienting; the hypnotic effect of the drum can lose its evocative power and jar you back into the conscious realm without any formal transition.

For this exercise, you will want to work within the construct of your magic circle.[20] You will be drawing the animal spirit from the psychic realm into the physical. Magical space becomes the enchanted ground for the forces of the Familiar, acting much as a lens through which one focuses the magical intent.

## SHAPESHIFTING MEDITATION

### WHAT YOU'LL NEED

- Your basic circle format (if you don't have a regular circle casting formula, one is provided in the back of this book)
- Shapeshifter incense[21]
- Water, salt, candle, incense (the basic circle construction tools)
- A drum or a drumming tape
- Your fetich

### TO BEGIN

Bless and consecrate your magic circle as usual, using the water, salt, candle, and incense. Light some of the shapeshifter incense at the start of the meditation. Find a comfortable sitting position in your circle and begin the drumming, followed by the meditation.

### DRUMMING THE POWER

Each animal power has its own drumbeat, which further changes in response to the specific need of the petitioner. Everyone feels the rhythms of the universe in their own way, so there is no set pattern or formula that says that certain beats draw certain animal powers. For instance, my drumbeat for Antelope would be different than yours. Also, because these powers are reflective of an ever-changing, fluid universe, the drumbeat at one moment might not be the same tomorrow, an hour from now, or perhaps even a minute from now. It is up to each magical worker to plug into the universal rhythms within, which in turn inform and lead the way.

## DISCOVERING THE DRUMBEAT

### Method 1

Hold the fetich over the smoking incense. Open your mind up to the Familiar consciousness. Watch the smoke for patterns and rhythms. If necessary, chant the name of your animal power as you watch. Slowly a pattern will emerge from the smoke and the drumbeat will be established.

### Method 2

Place the fetich in front of you. Take up your drum or rattle and begin a simple four-beat. Close your eyes and hold an image of your fetich within the mind's eye. Listen deep within your consciousness, and a pattern for a new beat will emerge. This is the drumbeat you will use for attracting the Familiar self.

### Method 3

Take your fetich to a spot outside where you can go relatively unobserved. Hold the fetich between the palms of your hands and listen to the noises around you: birds singing, dogs barking, automobile traffic, human voices, etc. Let these sounds form your rhythm.

## NEXT

Drum for at least a few minutes until you feel that the energies of the Familiar Self have been heightened. Once your energy is raised, once you feel a connection to the Familiar Self, begin the following meditation.

## THE MEDITATION

Turn on your tape recorder with the meditation below prerecorded, or if you have a partner, have the partner begin reading now. The reading should continue where the Beginning Exercise of chapter 1 leaves off:

**Reader:** As a blue mist swirls about your body, you begin to float. The swirling mist forms a shimmering globe around you that lifts you higher and higher. It takes you into the dream realm where you begin your sacred journey.

(**Reader** pause for a moment.)

The blue globe of mist now dissipates and reveals a moonlit sky. You are at a beach, at the base of some towering cliffs. Hear the distant waves crash. Watch them softly glide onto the shore. Gaze at the sea foam, glowing with phosphorescence beneath the silver light of the moon.

You move from the cliffs over to the water. As you approach, breathe in the clean, salty spray of the ocean. Bend down and touch the soft, wet sand while waiting for a gentle wave to wash toward you. When one comes, reach out, cup your hands, and take a handful of the water. Hold it up to the moonlight and say:

> MOTHER MOON, PROTECT ME WITH YOUR SILVERY LIGHT.

Look at the water cupped in your hands and you will notice that it has taken on a silver aura. Pour its silvery protective essence over your head. The silver aura surrounds and protects you now.

Your attention is caught by a small fire burning next to the cliffs. Go over to it. Once you are there, notice how the fire is surrounded by a circle of crystals implanted in the cool sand, with their shining spikes pointed skyward.

Seat yourself in the circle and watch the dancing flames of the fire. They are hypnotic and soon you are in an even deeper state of absorption. As you watch the fire, an indistinct image forms in its center. It begins to take the shape of a mask. The mask rises out of the fire. It is the mask of your spirit animal. Reach out, take the mask, and try it on.

The mask fits perfectly and snugly onto your features. After placing it on your face, you feel internal changes beginning to occur. Your senses are heightened as you see from the eyes of your animal spirit. Listen to the sounds of the night from its ears. Sniff the night air through its nose.

Now is the time to begin the magical dance within your new shape.

(**Reader:** pause now to allow the shapeshifter time to explore his or her new dimension through movement/dance. When the magical worker has danced for a while, you will notice the energies in the circle heighten. When you, the reader, sense that the magician has absorbed the energies sufficiently, begin the next portion of the exercise.)

**Reader:** It is time to begin your return to the outer realms. Sit where you are now. Take off the mask and let it float back to the bonfire, just above the flames. Watch it descend back into the place of its origin. It will be there any time you desire to use it. Step out of the circle now. Allow the blue globe of mist to surround you and lift you. You are coming back to the room, to a state of waking consciousness. You will, however, be changed from within.

You are back in your physical body now. As the mist begins to dissipate, open your eyes. Take a moment to adjust to your surroundings as you allow the experience you have just had to seep deeply into your psyche.

# JOURNALING

When you dance, are you able to let go any anxieties you might have had about your body and its movement?

In what ways can you see dance as being helpful to your spiritual growth?

Were you able to effect the transformation into the Familiar Self successfully?

What will make it more successful next time?

What was the feeling as you were completely immersed in the consciousness of the Familiar Self?

In what ways did you feel more empowered during the experience? In what ways were you less empowered?

## NOTES

1. Reginald Scot, *The Discoverie of Witchcraft* (Carbondale, IL: Southern Illinois University Press [London, 1584], 1964), 32.

2. Margaret Murray, *The God of the Witches* (1931. Reprint. New York: Oxford University Press, 1970), 24.

3. James G, Frazer, *The Golden Bough,* vol. 1 (New York: Avenel Books, [1890] 1981), 74.

4. Frazer, 80.

5. Hamilton A. Tyler, *Pueblo Animals and Myths* (Norman: University of Oklahoma Press, 1964), 69.

6. Marie Antoinette Czaplicka, *Aboriginal Siberia* (London: Oxford University Press, 1969), 236–8.

7. Murray, 145.

8. Jamake Highwater, *The Primal Mind: Vision and Reality in Indian America* (New York: Meridian Books, 1982), 135.

9. Highwater, 136.

10. Bernard F. Dukore, *Dramatic Theory and Criticism* (San Francisco: Duke Reinhart and Winston Inc., 1974), 843, excerpted from *The Spirit of Man, Art, and Literature,* ed. G. Adler, M. Fordham, and H, Read, trans. R.F.C. Hull (vol. 15 of *The Collected Works of C.G. Jung)* (Bollingen Series XX, 1966).

11. Mircea Eliade, *Shamanism: Archaic Techniques of Ecstasy,* trans. Willard R. Trask (New York: Pantheon Books, 1964), 385.

12. See, for example, John Matthews, *Taliesin; Shamanism and the Bardic Mysteries in Britain and Ireland* (Hammersmith, England: Aquarian Press, 1991).

13. Ford, 183–6.

14. Matthews, 152.

15. Eliade, 459.

16. Eliade, 460.

17. Patrick Ford, ed., *The Mabinogi and other Medieval and Welsh Tales* (Berkeley: University of California Press, 1977), 96, 97.

18. John Webster, *The Displaying of Supposed Witchcraft* (London: F.M., 1677), 175.

19. Eliade, 128, 129; Harner, 85.

20. See appendix for circle casting.

21. Again, this recipe is in the back of the book. However, you should use an incense blend that best speaks to your unconscious mind.

# *working with new animal powers*

The human inclination to adopt animals as spirit guides is evident in the totemic systems of people around the planet; these affiliations of kinship are believed to infuse the psyche with a variety of qualities, such as cunning, vision and strength.[1]

H aving mastered the previous exercises, we arrive at the culmination of our work with the Familiar Self. We will now begin to gain the powers of any of the animals we choose. The Familiar Self, as the core animal nature, works in harmony with other Familiar spirits. The core animal never changes. However, the core animal specializes in certain areas of personal development. When you as the Witch or shaman wish your personal development to take an alternative route, then another animal may be invoked.[2]

For instance, the weasel as a core animal can lend a quality of feistiness. However, there may be an occasion in which a feisty nature would not be completely useful. You as the magical worker may therefore wish to invoke (for example) the bear, a nurturing presence.

Invoking these new animal powers can markedly shift one's internal focus. This enables a shift in one's psychological profile to occur without losing the natural abilities of the core Familiar Self. The new animal power acts as a metaphor—a focus for changing consciousness. Whichever animals are internalized and identified with, this process creates new channels for drawing on internal resources that may have been previously difficult to attain.

# THE APPENDIX

Every animal power has its own gifts to bestow, which may range from psychic prowess to more tangible abilities, such as increased physical strength. These gifts are available to each of us. At the back of the book, you will find an appendix that lists some animals and their corresponding attributes. Use this a guide to selecting your new animal power. Some animals have similar attributes, but each has its own distinct way of teaching and imparting its power. You do not, however, want to work with more than one Familiar Spirit at a time. There is no particularly mystical reason for this. It is simply much more effective to focus on one goal or power at a time. If you try to incorporate too many aspects at once you will muddy the effect you had originally intended.

# THE NEW FAMILIAR RITE
## WHAT YOU WILL NEED

- Drum or rattle (or some other percussion instrument)
- Your new fetich (see below)
- Shapeshifter incense for the ritual/meditation
- A bowl of water
- A container of salt
- A green candle
- A partner to drum and read or an audiotape

This exercise works well with a partner who can drum while you work. If you're working alone, your drumming audiotape should last at least a good ten minutes. Have the tape cued up and accessible within the boundaries of your magic circle.

## MAKING A NEW FETICH

One of the first things we will need to do in the new totem rite is create an object that represents the spiritual power we seek. This is done through the process of creating a new fetich.

Listed below are several methods to creating the new power object.

### Method 1

Form the perimeter of a 15-inch diameter circle out of one or more of the following herbs: red clover, thistle, black hellebore, and juniper[3]— the traditional Witch herbs for animal blessings. (If you have a feline Familiar Power, catnip is always a good choice of herb!)

Place two white candles and Totem Spirit[4] incense in the middle of the circle, along with your original or core Familiar Self fetich. The fetich of the Familiar Self will aid you in your sacred vision. Light the incense and the candles now. Have the materials with which you plan to make the new fetich in the circle too.

Chant the name of the animal power you wish to invoke. For instance, if you were seeking the Dragon power, you would begin chanting "Dragon… Dragon … Dragon …" As you do this, cup the palms of your hands over the burning incense. Your hands will fill with smoke. Then turn your palms skyward, allowing the smoke to escape. Watch for designs, spirals, puffs, and so forth, all created by the smoking incense. Allow your mind to drift into Familiar consciousness, letting go of the conscious mind. When the unconscious takes over, you should be able to see forms and actual shapes appearing in the smoke. Keep repeating this process until the shape of your new fetich is evoked.

### Method 2

Look at photographs or drawings of the new animal you are seeking. Choose your favorite illustration or photo and place it within a 15-inch diameter circle formed with herbs sacred to the animal powers (listed in method 1). Close your eyes and while they remain closed use your modeling materials to reproduce the image you see in your mind's eye. This method produces some wonderful results because you are allowing the psychic senses to form the image. Once you close off the sense of mundane sight, you extend your ability to see deeper realities. Also, you are not judging your work when you have your eyes closed. This method allows art of the spontaneous self to emerge unhampered. Often some of the most interesting and visionary experiences come from this method.

Once you have made your new fetich, bless and consecrate it with the four elements as outlined in chapter 5. Once it is prepared, you can begin the New Familiar Rite.

## TO BEGIN

Light your incense and your candle. Place them in front of you. You now want to fortify your aura with protective light. Take in the element of Air from the incense, then proceed to Fire, Water, and Earth using the following rite. Afterward, you may cast your circle as usual.

## PROTECTIVE ELEMENTAL BLESSING

As was suggested earlier, when you work with animal powers other than your base animal, it is important to protect the psychic body. This is because you are inviting energies into your consciousness that may not normally be there. When asking new powers to enter your personal energy field, it is always a good idea to strengthen the aura and also ask for protection. Pick up the lit incense in its burner and face the East. Allow the incense to glide over you, visualizing a bright yellow light around your body. Breathe in the powers of the East, the powers of Air. Then say:

> KNOWLEDGE, THOUGHT, THE PLACE OF BEGINNINGS. O
> MIGHTY ONES OF AIR, GUIDE AND PROTECT ME WITH
> THY WISDOM. I AM PROTECTED BY THE ELEMENT OF AIR.

After using the incense, pick up the lit candle and face the South. Visualize the flame of the candle emitting a bright red light that covers your entire body. Imagine the heat of the Sun. Take in the power of Fire, the element of the South. Again, when you are ready to begin, say:

WILL, ENERGY, THE BURNING POINT OF OVERWHELM-
ING PASSION. O MIGHTY ONES OF FIRE, PROTECT ME
WITH STRENGTH OF BODY AND MIND. I AM PROTECTED
BY THE ELEMENT OF FIRE.

Next take the bowl of water. Face the West. Touch a few of the
cooling droplets to your lips and brow. Imagine a bright blue aura surrounding your body now. Visualize an ocean shore. Waves roll up the
shore and sea foam laps around your ankles. Take in the powers of
Water, the element of the West, and say:

EMOTIONS, INTUITION, CYCLES, THE PLACE OF END-
INGS. O MIGHTY ONES OF WATER, PROTECT ME WITH
YOUR POWERS OF INSIGHT. I AM PROTECTED WITH THE
ELEMENT OF WATER.

Take the container of salt or earth and face the North. Touch a dab
of salt to the third eye and see a bright green aura surrounding you.
Visualize a cold, rocky mountainside looming before you on a moonless
night. Take in the element of Earth, the power of the North, and say:

STABILITY, SILENCE, THE DARK, RICH MOTHER-WOMB.
O MIGHTY ONES OF THE NORTH, PROTECT ME WITH
THY WISDOM AND MYSTERY. I AM PROTECTED BY THE
ELEMENT OF EARTH.

Cast a magic circle.

Using your drum (or other percussion instrument), begin drumming in a simple three- or four-beat rhythm until you feel a shift from
ordinary to Familiar consciousness take place.

## CALLING UP THE TOTEM

Once you feel you are in an altered state, take the sacred image of your
new totem in your hands and present it to the four quarters. Start first
in the East, the place of beginning, and say:

> I CALL TO THEE, MY SACRED POWER! I SUMMON THEE
> FROM THE EAST AND ALL AIRY PLACES. BE PRESENT IN
> MY CIRCLE NOW, YE MIGHTY (NAME OF ANIMAL). BRING
> TO ME THE POWERS OF (SPEAK THE ESSENCE OF ANIMAL
> POWER YOU DESIRE).

Next to the South:

> I CALL TO THEE, MY SACRED POWER! I SUMMON THEE
> FROM THE SOUTH AND ALL FIERY PLACES. BE PRESENT
> IN MY CIRCLE NOW, YE MIGHTY (NAME OF ANIMAL).
> BRING TO ME THE POWERS OF (SPEAK THE ESSENCE OF
> ANIMAL POWER YOU DESIRE).

Next to the West:

> I CALL TO THEE, MY SACRED POWER! I SUMMON THEE
> FROM THE WEST AND ALL WATERY PLACES. BE PRESENT
> IN MY CIRCLE NOW, YE MIGHTY (NAME OF ANIMAL).
> BRING TO ME THE POWERS OF (SPEAK THE ESSENCE OF
> ANIMAL POWER YOU DESIRE).

Now to the North:

> I CALL TO THEE, MY SACRED POWER! I SUMMON THEE
> FROM THE NORTH AND ALL EARTHY PLACES. BE PRE-
> SENT IN MY CIRCLE NOW, YE MIGHTY (NAME OF ANI-
> MAL). BRING TO ME THE POWERS OF (SPEAK THE
> ESSENCE OF ANIMAL POWER YOU DESIRE).

## CATCHING IN THE FETICH

Catching the Familiar is the magical act of using the fetich to contain the animal power. The fetich acts like a link or a conduit for the power of the Familiar. The first step in the catching rite is drumming the new animal's power.

Once you have the beat established, feel a link beginning to form between you and the new Familiar Spirit. Once you have a clear mental image of the power animal, you will now begin to incorporate it into your fetich.

Visualize the animal spirit entering the fetich. The fetich will hold the animal power until you are ready to dance the animal. Once you feel the new energy of the animal inside the figurine, commence the shapeshifting meditation and dance.

## DANCING THE ANIMAL

Next, you should dance the new animal just as was done in the shapeshifting exercise of chapter 8.

As you do the meditation before the dance, hold the fetich containing the animal power to your heart chakra. Allow the presence of the animal to filter into your psyche from the figure. Hold the fetich only until you feel the new essence fill you.

Turn on the drumming tape, or have a partner begin drumming. At that point you should set the fetich down and begin to trancedance, enacting the movements and gestures of the new animal power. Dancing the animal helps to set this new power within in motion.

## AFTER THE DANCE

Take time to ground yourself after the ritual. This may include eating, drinking, stomping your feet, or holding your hands to the floor to release the excess energy. You don't want to be "floating around" all day on the excess energy you may have raised.

Lastly, thank the Universe for providing you with what you needed. Then close and dismantle the circle.

## THE CEREMONY OF RETURN

Within several days of the New Totem Rite, give the animal spirit thanks and send it off to help another person. Though the new Familiar Spirit is gone, it will have left behind its power. This is because you have internalized it to make it your own.

# WHAT YOU WILL NEED

- Your new totem fetich
- A red candle
- A bowl of water
- A dish of rock salt
- Incense

Cast a magic circle. Hold the fetich over the smoldering incense and spiritually cleanse it with Air, saying:

> I BID THEE GO!
> WITH THE POWER TO KNOW!

Now, hold it over the flickering candle light saying:

> YOUR TASK FULFILLED,
> WITH THE POWER TO WILL!

Now sprinkle the fetich with water saying:

> RETURN TO THY LAIR,
> WITH THE POWER TO DARE!

Place the fetich in the rock salt, covering it completely, saying:

> FAREWELL, THIS HOUR,
> O SILENT POWER!

Close your circle, leaving the fetich in the salt. After three days have passed, remove the fetich from the salt and keep it with your other sacred objects.

## NOTES

1. Adele Getty, *Goddess, Mother of Living Nature* (London: Thames and Hudson Ltd., 1990), 80.

2. We do not, however, want to work with more than one Familiar Spirit at a time. There is no particularly mystical reason for this. It is simply much more effective to focus on one goal or power at a time. If you try to incorporate too many aspects at once you will muddy the effect you had originally intended.

3. These are herbs traditionally connected with animal magic and the blessing of animals. See, for example, Paul Beryl, *The Master Book of Herbalism* (Custer, Washington: Phoenix Publishing, 1984), 222, 232, 243, 250.

4. Again, the recipe is in the back of the book. However, be sure to use an incense that best speaks to your unconscious mind.

# *healing animals*

A witch told a [sick] girl that she must keep a nine days fast
. . . on the night of the last day, the witch died in prison;
but nevertheless the girl was shortly afterwards healed, having voided by the back passage several little animals in the
form of lizards, as the witch had told her.
— Henrey Boguet, *An Examen of Witches*[1]

## ECSTATIC HEALING

Healing has always been one of the tasks of the shaman in traditional societies. Wild Witches, as the shamans of Northern Europe, have also historically assumed the role of healer.[2] Many modern Witches engage in the study of one form of healing or another. The healing methods employed by magical folk are usually based on the concept that healing must occur in a natural cycle in order to be sound and complete. Therefore, most Witches prefer holistic methods of health promotion. Time-honored forms of healing for contemporary Witches range from tangible methods such as herbalism, psychological counseling, and laying on of hands to abstract, spiritual systems such as spellcraft and auric healing.[3]

Here is an ecstatic, wild Witch method for healing with the aid of your Familiar Self. As usual, you will need a partner to drum for you or a drumming tape.

# TECHNIQUE

Cast a magic circle. Blindfold your patient and lay him or her down in the center of your circle.

If your patient has done work with animal spirits, ask what his or her Familiar Spirit is. If the patient does not know, continue on to the next step and allow the experience to inform you. It is not important to know beforehand which animal to call, because sometimes the patient has changed animal teachers without knowing that it has happened. In fact, this internal transition is sometimes the reason for an illness. This transition is sometimes due to "soul loss," which usually happens when people lose track of their spiritual path.[4] When the animal spirit wanders, its service is no longer needed. The new animal teacher wants to get the attention of the student, and of course, the animal speaks through the body.

Kneel down next to the patient and place your hands over his or her heart chakra (the center of the chest, just above the breastbone).[5] Open yourself up to the energies of the patient's animal spirit.

Close your eyes, and with your hands still over the heart center, follow the shapeshifting meditation as described in chapter 8. The only difference will come when you see the mask emerging from the flames; expect to see the mask of the patient's animal helper.

Here you must incorporate physical movement and visualization. As you visualize the animal mask of your patient, reach out with your physical hands and grab it. You may actually feel its astral body. Physically place the animal spirit mask on the patient while visualizing it affixing to his or her face. Sit once again, this time facing your patient. With your eyes closed, imagine your animal mask emerging from the flames. Once again, reach out with your physical hands and take the mask. Place it on your face and imagine the animal shift beginning to take place. At this point, you should do the shapeshifting dance to evoke fully the essence of your Familiar consciousness.

Once you feel your own animal's energy, focus within. Physically hold your hands over the patient's heart, which in traditional lore is the place where the Familiar Self resides. Mentally ask your animal the location of the patient's illness as well as its cause. Ask what steps need to be taken by the patient, either physical or spiritual, to begin the healing process. Once you have received the message, you can remove your hands from the patient's heart center and sit facing him or her once again.

Once you have completed this, you are ready to return to the conscious realm. Be sure to allow the patient time to absorb any energies released by the rite. Explain what his or her animal spirit has told you along with any instructions given to speed up the healing process.

The challenge of this healing method lies in the balance between the inner and outer worlds and the healer's ability to work with one foot planted firmly on the grounds of each. On the one hand, the healer must be able to concentrate on his or her inner world and the transference of power (or the patient's animal mask) to the patient. On the other hand the healer needs to have the ability to use her or his physical hands, and have the ability to relay the healing messages of the Familiar Self. This is not necessarily an easy task. You should practice this technique often so that you will have the skill to move easily between the worlds of spirit and matter.

# JOURNALING

How did the patient respond to the magical healing?

Did the person you were working with allow the flow of energy between you and their animal spirit or did you find it difficult to pass energy?

Were you as the healer able to effectively stay balanced between the worlds of spirit and matter?

So that you'll remember the feeling for future work—what were the differences in energy you felt between the worlds?

Was the patient's illness due to "soul loss?" If so, what was the previous Familiar Self of the patient, and what is the new Familiar Self?

## NOTES

1. Henrey Boguet, *An Examen of Witches* (Great Britain: John Rodker, 1929. Reprint. New York: Barnes & Nobles, 1971), 109.

2. Janet and Stewart Farrar, *The Witches' Way* (London: Robert Hale, 1984), 220.

3. See, for example, Farrar, 220–234.

4. Jamake Highwater, *The Primal Mind: Vision and Reality in Indian America* (New York: Meridian Books, 1982), 135.

5. Simply put, the chakras are the seven principal energy centers of the human body. The first is located at the base of the spine at the rectum, the second is located at the regenerative organs, the third is in the solar plexus, the fourth is at the heart, the fifth is at the base of the throat, the sixth is on the brow between the eyes, and the seventh is at the crown of the head. Each chakra is connected with specific kinds of energy. See, for example, Anodea Judith, *Wheels of Life: A Users Guide to the Chakra System* (St. Paul, Minnesota: Llewellyn Publications, 1990).

# SECTION 3

## *the physical familiar*

# *domestic familiars*

p until now our work has centered around the "spirit" aspect of the Familiar. We have learned of the powers of the animal spirits living within each of us. Our journey does not end here. At this point we turn to the animal that lives with the Witch: the physical Familiar.

Animals are sacred. They are living expressions of the divine principle—the Goddess and God manifest in living form. Seeking communion with living creatures and the natural world is the heritage of the Witch. It is important for us to interact with animals on the level of spirit—regarding these creatures as physical Familiars—because doing so tunes us into the natural tides of the Gods.

Since we view the animal world as sacred, we need to take certain precautions when working with Familiars. Because it is my belief that those reading this book intend to work with animals in only safe, non-threatening ways, I have provided general groundrules to consider before engaging in the physical Familiar work to come.

# THE FIVE BASIC GROUNDRULES

These are the five basic groundrules for working with animals in a magical setting. Each rule will be explored in more depth throughout the following chapters, but for now, take a moment to review this overview.

1. Only work with animals that are willing to work with you.

2. Never bind, cage, leash, or restrict the movement of an animal during magical operations.

3. Allow your Familiars to come and go from the magical space as they please.

4. Never use candles or incense around animals, as there is too much risk of harming them. The replacement for fire is the alchemical symbol for Fire:

   Color the symbol bright red to add magical potency. Also note that the standard symbolic tool for Fire, in traditional Wicca, is the athame (a black-handled, doubled-edged knife). However, for obvious safety reasons, the use of a knife around animals should never be considered. Likewise, it is strongly advised never to take other sharp instruments into a ritual setting with a physical Familiar.

   The replacement for incense, the symbolic tool for Air, is the wand, or even a gentle bell.

5. Be certain to cover ritual herbs and foods that could be harmful to your Familiar.

## THE DOMESTIC FAMILIAR

The Familiar is commonly thought of as any type of magical animal in the service of a Witch. The actual, physical animal presence is the second type of Familiar which Margaret Murray called the "domestic familiar."

This latter aspect is the one that has been impressed on our consciousness since birth and with which most people hold their most immediate associations—a black cat or some other nocturnal creature riding on the broomstick of a greeting-card Halloween witch. While purists consider such images vulgarizations, they linger on in mass consciousness precisely because they do, in fact, touch profoundly upon primal archetypes. The Familiar's image has been retained in popular culture because, just like myth and fairy tale, it is an image born from the womb of truth. What it reveals to us is the sense, however dim, that animals have been and always will be powerful magical partners. The physical Familiar is a genuine artifact of a tradition which also lingers within deep consciousness: the Wiccan path.

Physical animal presences represent the life force in an unfettered state. When we observe animals, we see that they act out of the drives of the natural forces within them. Since Witches strive to connect with their liberated, spiritual consciousness, they naturally align with physical Familiars, viewing them as models and teachers for their life journeys. Many Witches feel that their households would not be complete without animal presences to guard, protect, and bless them, and will attest to the fact that some animals delight in their magical workings. Indeed, animals and magic go hand in hand. Animals are naturally attuned to magic and it is to the benefit of any serious magical practitioner to develop a rapport with a domestic Familiar. Traditionally, the operations that optimally utilize the Familiar's powers are healing, wishing, protection, and psychic empowerment. Probably these were the traditional provinces of the domestic Familiar because these were the most common requests brought before the village wise woman or man. The domestic Familiar's magical abilities, of course, extend far beyond the traditional limitations and can add spiritual enrichment to any aspect of the modern Witch's work.

Less than 200 years ago, of course, the physical Familiar was not commonly regarded as an animal associated with such benign workings. Since at least the beginnings of the Witch persecutions, the domestic Familiar has routinely been abused.

The standard text used by the Church in the 16th century for finding and punishing Witches was the *Malleus Malificarum,* which maligned domestic animals as demonic presences. Consequently, people could be suspected of Witchcraft simply because they kept domestic animals or showed an affinity for them.

History as well as common sense tells us that most of those accused of Witchcraft were wholly ignorant of any real magical knowledge. Some, however, did evince an understanding of the magical capabilities of animals. Within the testimonies extracted from the persecuted, there appears to be an awareness of Familiar magic similar to the animal lore extant among certain contemporary shamanic peoples. For instance, when questioned by authorities, some of the alleged Witches claimed that their domestic animals came to them from their Gods. The idea of God-given animal helpers is found in the modern shamanic beliefs of the native North Americans, the Jivaro of Eastern Ecuador, the Inuit, and many Australian aboriginals.[1] Those suspected of Witchcraft sometimes claimed that the animals would do tasks for them, just as the contemporary shamans claim.

When considering that numerous cultures around the world have made use of the Familiar, it is not difficult to imagine that magical powers have been attributed to nearly every kind of creature. It is interesting to observe how physical geography and culture have influenced which animals are considered to be the animals of power. A physical Familiar must on no account be confused with the animal that actually lives with a Witch or shaman, known as a domestic Familiar. In the non-Western cultures, the physical animal presences thought of as powerful creatures are nondomesticated animals. In some native North American tribes, for example, the eagle, bear, wolf, and beaver are commonly mentioned physical Familiar animals. Among the Siberian shamans, the physical animal powers are seagulls and wolves. The shamans along the Amazon see jaguars and snakes as Familiar animals. Inuit see ravens, wolves, polar bears, and seals as Familiars. Compared to the more exotic animals of other traditional peoples, the Witch's Familiar historically appears to be the most easily domesticated. Witches commonly thought personal animals of power were cats, ferrets, small birds, dogs, and cows, to name just a few.[2]

Witches after all, were (and still are) concerned with acquiring the ability to bend and shape the energies of nature. Having a domesticated animal in their presence allowed them more insight into the tides and powers of nature. Another interesting point is that most other native cultures historically rarely kept the physical animal powers in their presence, yet the Western shamanic tradition encouraged this. Because Western values are so tainted by Christianity, we are acculturated to think that we are separate from nature. No doubt, the early Witches tried to break this pattern of thought by actually living with nature, the plants, the animals, and all wild things.

The physical form of the animal powers may change from culture to culture, but the purpose of the animal as magical helper and guide remains the same: each is a focus for connecting with our own inner power resource—and for connecting to the traditions of our wild Witch ancestors.

The following chapters offer an exploration of the magical gifts provided by the physical Familiar, as well as how to acquire, consecrate and empower one.

## NOTES

1. Michael J. Harner, *The Way of the Shaman* (New York: Bantam, 1980), 74–6.

2. Doreen Valiente, *An ABC of Witchcraft* (New York: St. Martin's Press, 1973), 153, According to many testimonies, these animals were typically black.

# the making of a familiar

hoosing the right Familiar for yourself is a challenging and rewarding task. Some points that prospective animal magic workers should think about before the selection of a domestic Familiar include:

Is the expense of a domestic animal feasible? Remember, vaccinations, food, grooming supplies, and licensing are just a few of the standard animal expenditures.

Think about your accommodations. Does your home provide enough windows, light, and fresh air for a domestic Familiar? Is there adequate space to house a domestic Familiar? Obviously, if you are living in a one-room apartment in a complex that does not allow pets, it would be unrealistic to embark on training.

Is there already a domestic animal in your life? If so, consider the possibility of working with it. This is not to say that every domestic animal will want to participate in magical work, but some definitely will. If you already live with an animal you feel is unsuitable for magical partnership and you therefore wish to train another one, consider that it will need to be compatible with the one(s) you already have.

There is an old tradition governing the acquisition of a Familiar: a Familiar must be inherited from another Witch. A contemporary adaptation of this tradition dictates that one never "buy" an animal for magical purposes. The reason, I suspect, is that no one can really "own" another life form. Paying money for just that purpose seems to take the magical charge out of an animal.

With this in mind, the local animal shelter makes the best hunting ground for potential domestic Familiars. You may have to pay a small fee at the pound, but this covers the cost of vaccinations, staff, food provision, and keeping the public facility open as a refuge for neglected or lost domestic animals. The fee is not to "buy" another life form.

## FOR PEOPLE WHO ALREADY HAVE A PET THEY WISH TO MAKE THEIR FAMILIAR

Your pet, of course, must first make his/her wishes to participate in your magical endeavors known. Since your pet cannot verbalize (forgive me if I am mistaken), observe its body language. Animals have ways of letting us know what they want. All you need is sensitivity to the possibilities inherent in their body language. Most pet owners already know their pets' language and can respond accordingly.

Consider, for example, the signals that a cat gives when it wants to go outside; these are not mysterious. Usually the animal will sit near the door and scratch at it. Another example is the dog who displays "begging" behaviors at meal times; staring at the food and licking its chops are enough to indicate that it wants food. Likewise, when trying to discover whether or not your pet wants to be your magical partner, consider its nonverbal communication on the subject. Look for signs of "Familiarship" in your domestic entity:

- Does your pet like to join you in your magic circle? Or does it avoid your circle?

- Does your pet make its sleeping place on/under/near your magical supplies? Or does it shy away from them?

- Does your pet get excited at the beginning of a ceremony? Or does it go off into some corner and go to sleep?

- If you leave your magical tools out, will your pet explore or play with them? Or does it leave them alone?

If you have observed two or more positive behaviors on more than one occasion, your animal is a likely Familiar candidate. If not, don't worry; your domestic animal may be "normal," but that doesn't mean it cannot or will not lend power to your magical workings. A domestic animal's mere presence adds power to magic.

# THE CALL

One way to bring a magical animal presence into your life is to first announce your magical intentions on the astral plane. This is done through the ritual of the Call. This is a good rite to perform if you already have a domestic animal you would like to include in your magical workings, or if you have a particular animal you're considering after some searching.

The purpose of performing the Call is to test the magical waters first. You want to make certain that your animal wants to participate with you on a spiritual level.

## WHAT YOU'LL NEED

- The usual tools to construct a magic circle
- Totem Spirit incense
- A deck of Tarot cards
- A small brown candle with the name of the animal inscribed upon it

Cast your circle as usual.[1]
Use dancing or drumming to raise magical energy.[2]
After dancing and drumming, when you have enough energy raised, light up some of the Shapeshifter incense. Light the brown candle as well.
Close your eyes and imagine your potential Familiar in front of you. If you have a photograph of the animal, hold it between your hands and say:

THE BEASTS ARE CALLED
BY MY WILL AND BY ALL WHO
DANCE TO RHYTHMS TREAD BY FEW.
TO HOOVES AND BRAYING FLAMES
OF ANCIENT SONG ARE BEAT
ON SKINS OF THE HUNTED
DEEP ON MOONLESS NIGHTS.
COME TO THE CALL! COME TO THE DANCE,
CREATURES OF THE EARTH AND STARS!

Continue to imagine your animal before you. Ask if it wants to help you and wait for the psychic response. Sometimes the answer comes in words. Sometimes the animal gives a visual cue on the psychic level. Sometimes the answer will come later in a dream. Finally, know that the response may come on the physical level; the animal may join you in the circle. Wait, listen, watch, and be aware.

In some cases there may be no response on either the psychic or physical level. This is a sign that the animal does not want to participate in your magical work.

If your domestic animal does not respond physically (by entering the circle or making noises at the time of the Call), but agrees in your meditation to do magical work—or vice versa—consider the Tarot divination described below as a backup means of response. However, if one method says yes and the other says no, delay the dedication of your animal. After some days have passed, go ahead and try the Call ritual again.

Be patient and open to the possibilities. If the answer is yes on all levels, go on to the dedication ceremony.

## TAROT DIVINATION FOR THE FAMILIAR

Misinterpretation can happen. After all, little Scruffy entered your circle, he might have been trying to tell you all along that he needed to go wee-wee outside. But being the good magical worker that you are, you read your animal's body language and construed his presence as a sign of psychic prowess. The easiest way to avoid such errors is to consult a divinatory oracle, such as the Tarot, as part of your Call rite.

This is an accurate method and needs to be performed only once to get the answer. It's not always a good idea to try the "two out of three" method of divination. Be satisfied with the resulting answer, regardless of the outcome. After all, an animal no more wants to be forced into magical work than you want to be coerced into activities that are uncomfortable for you.

To begin the Tarot reading, hold the deck over the candle flame and again visualize the animal before you. Imagine you touch your animal between the eyes. (By the way, animals do have psychic sensitivity centers, one of which is similar to our third eye.) While mentally contacting your animal this way, ask this question aloud:

> DO YOU WISH TO ASSIST ME IN MAGICAL WORK AS A
> FAMILIAR, APPRENTICE, AND HELPER?

Shuffle the cards with this question in mind. When you sense it is time to stop shuffling, spread them out face down and select any three. Turn them over and lay them in a row from left to right.

## INTERPRETATION

If two or three cards are right side up (picture is right side up, facing you), the answer is yes.

If two or three cards are reversed (picture is upside down, facing away from you), then the answer is no.

To enhance the reading, or to obtain greater details as to why the answer is yes or no, apply this formula to the existing card layout:

- Card One = Past
- Card Two = Present
- Card Three = Future

Card One, or the card of the past, shows the foundation of the question. It shows past situations that have led to the answer. Card Two represents the present and shows the current attitude of the animal toward magical work. Card Three indicates the future of the work with your Familiar.[3]

## CLOSING THE CIRCLE

After you have your response, end your magic circle. Be sure to let the brown candle burn all the way down after the ritual. This will help attract a different animal if you received a "no" answer, and it will bless and protect the "yes" answer.

# NOW WHAT?

After you have completed the divinatory process, and assuming the answer was a resounding yes, it is time to proceed with the dedication ceremony.

Below are listed some practical guidelines for work with the animal not only in the dedication ceremony, but in the context of all rites involving the presence of the physical Familiar. Remember that animals are free spirits and sometimes are not aware of simple dangers. For this reason, you must take care to remove as much of that element as you can from the circles in which you involve the animal.

Some general rules for working with a pet in the dedication circle and thereafter are:

- Always treat your Familiar with respect and dignity. Never, ever, force an animal to participate in your rites. Animals will usually let you know if they want to help you or not.

- If your Familiar leaves during the dedication ceremony, allow it to go. Never manipulate an animal in any way to stay within the circle. Before the dedication, it's a good idea to make a fetich that represents your physical Familiar. This you can use in place of the animal in the event he or she decides to wander outside of the ritual space.

- Never let your Familiar get too close to an open flame or dripping candle wax. It is very difficult to get candle wax out of animal fur; you may end up having to cut it off. Use covered, votive candles in your ceremonies.

- Cover all ritual food before you begin; otherwise you may not have your celebratory meal for later! Also cover sharp objects and any cutting utensils you might use. Keep loose incense in a covered container, or your Familiar may get a nose full of snuff! Be as cautious in your circle as if you had a child present and your Familiar will stay safe.

## NAMING THE FAMILIAR

Before you commence with the dedication ceremony, you will want to have a magical name for your Familiar. This means that your Familiar will now have two names: a mundane one and a magical one. Magical names are important in the Craft of the Wise. Proverbial wisdom says that to know the name of something is to have power over it. The point is to keep the magical name of the Familiar a secret.

Even writing down a magical name can take power away from it. If you must, only tell one or two friends whom you can trust to keep a secret the magical name of anything. Some historical Familiar names are: Pyewacket, Tom Twit, Bunne, Newes, Pygine, Prickeare, Vinegar Tom, Tissey, Greedigut, Greymalkin, Lightfoot, and Blackman. The appropriate time to call the Familiar by the magical name is when you draw upon his or her power in magic.

# DEDICATION RITUAL

## WHAT YOU'LL NEED

- A red candle
- Some sage or mint leaves
- Wand (or bell)
- Salt
- Water
- A fetich of your Familiar
- Oil
- A white candle (with the animal's magical name inscribed)

Cast a magic circle. After this is done, stand facing the East. Use your athame to cut out of the circle. Be certain to cover your athame and place it safely away before allowing your animal into the circle. Usher your Familiar in and close the circle. If the animal leaves at any time, resume the rite using the fetich you made prior to the circle.

Present the animal to the four quarters. You begin in the East, saying:

> MIGHTY ONES OF THE EAST,
> SEE BEFORE YOU THY MAGICAL BEAST
> _____ (animal's mundane name), READY TO
> BE MADE A FAMILIAR.

Moving clockwise, take the animal to the South:

> MIGHTY ONES OF THE SOUTH,
> FLAMES BURST FORTH FROM THE SNOUT AND MOUTH
> OF _____, READY TO BE MADE A FAMILIAR.

Now move to the West still holding your animal:

> MIGHTY ONES OF THE WEST,
> HERE, SUCKLED BY THE MOTHER'S BREAST,
> IS _____, READY TO BE MADE A FAMILIAR.

Finally, present the animal in the North:

> MIGHTY ONES OF THE NORTH,
> GNOMES HAVE ALREADY SUMMONED FORTH
> _____, READY TO BE MADE A FAMILIAR.

Take some sage or mint leaves, dip them in your consecrated salt and water mixture, and lightly sprinkle the animal, saying:

> EARTH AND WATER,
> WATER AND EARTH,
> AID _____ (Familiar's name)
> IN (HIS/HER) SPIRITUAL BIRTH!

Take the wand and wave it over your Familiar.[4] Light the red candle and hold it toward your Familiar saying:

> FIRE AND AIR,
> AIR AND FIRE,
> LEAD _____ (Familiar's name)
> IN THE GOD'S DESIRE!

Next, read the following invocation with your hands outstretched over the animal:

> AS ONCE WAS DONE IN CERRIDWEN'S NAME,
> THE CAULDRON WOMB IS SET AFLAME.
> AND FROM ITS DEPTHS IS FOUND REBIRTH,
> AND KNOWLEDGE FROM OUR MOTHER EARTH.
> CONJURE WELL THE GRAND ASSAY
> FAMILIAR ART THOU FROM THIS DAY!
> BY MOON AND SUN—BY LAND AND SEA,
> THY PATH AWAITS, SO MOTE IT BE!

Put some oil on your index finger and anoint the animal on the brow or chest region, saying:

> I CONSECRATE THEE A FAMILIAR AND LIVING EXPRESSION OF MAGIC!

Anoint your white, inscribed candle with the same oil. Then light the candle as a symbol of the beginning of your work with the new Familiar, saying:

> BE THOU KNOWN AMONG THE GODS AND WISE ONES
> AS _____ (new magical name), A LIVING ELEMENTAL AND CREATURE OF THE TWO WORLDS!

Present your dedicated Familiar to the four quarters. If the animal has left your circle, present the lighted white candle and the fetich at each of the quarters, saying:

COME YE SYLPHS OF THE EAST!
BEFORE YOU STANDS_____,
A NEWLY CONSECRATED FAMILIAR.

COME YE SALAMANDERS OF THE SOUTH!
BEFORE YOU STANDS_____,
A NEWLY CONSECRATED FAMILIAR.

COME YE UNDINES OF THE WEST!
BEFORE YOU STANDS_____,
A NEWLY CONSECRATED FAMILIAR.

COME YE GNOMES OF THE NORTH!
BEFORE YOU STANDS _____,
A NEWLY CONSECRATED FAMILIAR.

As a celebratory meal, you can share some cakes with your new Familiar either within the circle at this time or after the circle. This is your formal grounding of the magical energy raised.

Close the circle as usual.

# NOTES

1. Never leave lit candles or smoldering incense where your pet can disturb them. Always observe "Safe Ritual." Also, never force the animal to be in the room with you by leashing or caging it. Simply bring the animal into the room at the time of the ritual; it it leaves, simply allow it. Animals have the uncanny ability to move into and out of a magical space without breaking its energy. I was once told "animals and fools (meaning true innocents) can move through the magic circle without breaking its flow." Use the fetich instead of the animal when necessary and appropriate.

2. If your pet is afraid of the loud noise the drums make, skip it! Use chanting or meditation to get into an altered state.

3. Consult Eden Grey's *The Tarot Revealed* (New York: Signet Books, 1969) for interpretations of the cards.

4. Remember that some animals are afraid of smoke. It is best to use the wand as your symbolic representation of Air.

# *a blessing for non-familiars*

One of the usual functions of shamans and Witches is the blessing of animals. Witches and shamans were traditionally called in to heal sick livestock, to midwife for various animals during labor, to add protective energy to shield the animals from danger for the coming year, and to fashion charms to insure their fertility.

One interesting note is that the Church, which was so adamant about its policies regarding animals and their "obvious" link to Satan, eventually adopted a positive view of animals. When the Church fathers had sufficiently driven Witches and shamans underground, the clergy took over their role, creating their own animal blessing rituals and depicting various saints as champions of the animal powers. In modern Catholicism, the most popular animal-oriented saint, of course, is Francis of Assisi, who was reputed to have the ability to draw wild animals to him and magically tame them.

Any animal in the life of a magical worker should be blessed and protected. Animals, after all, bestow their own forms of blessing to you every day. Think of a dog who sits in your lap to lick your hand or face; canine saliva carries natural antibiotics that the dog uses in self-healing. It is offering healing energy and, of course, love to you—whether you realize it or not!

Domestic animals trust you just as children trust their parents; they depend on you to protect, provide, and guard them. Blessing the animal is a way of spiritually extending this security. As with all blessings, this should be done with the elements of Air, Fire, Water, and Earth; and in this case, summoning the old Celtic animal deities Epona (Eh-PO-nuh) and Cernunnos (Ker-NOON-os) is also appropriate.

Of course, invoking the ancient nature Gods actively stirs within us the wild callings of our Pagan antiquity. Evoking their names is not done merely as an antiquarian gesture, but rather to rouse archetypes that lie deep within our collective unconscious. In this way the Gods are not merely names, ideas, and symbols; they are the spirits of powerful forces residing in each of us.

With this in mind, we call upon our protective powers in the name of Epona. In Celtic mythology, she appears as the Horse Goddess.[1] Epona has ties to the Irish Macha and Dagda, or "Good God,"[2] as well as to the Greek Demeter[3] and in general to the bountiful Mother of all things.[4] She appears in the *Mabinogion* as the character Rhiannon.[5] The representations of the Goddess Epona are the horse and the cornucopia.[6]

Cernunnos is most widely known as the Celtic Lord of the Beasts.[7] He is the Horned God of animals, nature, and fecundity.[8] It has been speculated that Cernunnos appears in the Welsh Mythic epic, the *Mabinogion,* as the character Conall Cernach.[9] The famous Gundestrap Cauldron, found in Gundestrap, Denmark (in a peat bog), depicts an antlered Cernunnos sitting cross-legged among the animals.[10]

When we bless in their names, we bless with the power of forces that connect us to the wild. These deities remind us that we are neither superior nor inferior to the other animals. Rather, we are all strands in a complex, interconnected web of life energy.

# BLESSING RITUAL

## WHAT YOU WILL NEED

- Eight stones or crystals

*Epona*

- Blessing oil
- Water
- Salt
- Bell
- A Fire symbol: △

It will not be necessary to bless your non-Familiar animals within the construct of your magic circle.

You can do this ritual during either sunlight or moonlight hours.[11] In either case, it is best to consecrate animals while the Moon is in a waxing or full cycle. Check an almanac, your magical calendar, or even the daily newspaper to find out when the Moon will be either waxing or, ideally, full.

Take time beforehand to consider the influences of the luminary with which you will be working. Some Wiccan traditions suggest that men work with the energies of the Sun, which is a symbol of divine masculinity, and that women work with the Moon, which is sacred to all of womanhood. When a Witch works within the framework of this type of energy system, she or he is thought to be working alongside the natural energy flows of the planet.

Other traditions prefer working with polarity. In other words, women work with the Sun and men with the Moon tides. Working with the polarity system is said to generate psychic power. Try working with both systems. It is always better to perform rituals in the manner that best suits you.

If you are intending to bless by the light of the waxing Moon, call upon the presence of the Lady Epona. She protects the animals with a silvery lunar aura. If you plan to work by the light of the Sun, evoke the name of the Lord Cernunnos. He will protect the animals with a golden, solar aura.

## ANIMAL BLESSING CIRCLE

### Draw your circle

Go to an outdoor space and find a stick. Use it to draw a circle in the earth. The diameter of your circle should be just big enough to fit the length of the largest animal you intend to bless. Once this is done you will place the stones or crystals around you, forming the perimeter of your circle. For this, you will go around the circle twice. The first time, you will place only four of the stones: first in the North, then in the East, South, and then in the West. The second time around, you will place the remaining four stones in between the first four starting in the Northeast, then the Southeast, Southwest, and finally in the Northwest. As you place each stone, say:

> I START IN THE NORTH AND CIRCLE 'ROUND.
> I END IN THE NORTH FOR HOLY GROUND.

Once this is completed, hold your arms out to the sky. Take in the power of the Sun or Moon, saying:

> BLESSED _____ (Epona or Cernunnos),
> BE FAVORABLE UPON MY RITE,
> CAST ROUND THIS CIRCLE
> WITH THE POWER OF YOUR (SUN/MOON) LIGHT.

## Elemental blessing

Since this is not a standard magical circle, you can move within and without with no disturbance of the psychic energy field. You can now leave to bring an animal into the circle. Consecrate the animal with each element by touching a bit of each to the animal's hide.[12] While doing so, say:

> BLESSED    THOU    BE    WITH    THE    MIGHT    OF
> _____ (AIR, FIRE, WATER, EARTH).[13]

## God/dess blessing

Take a dab of oil and apply it to the brow of the animal. If done in the moonlight, anoint with the sign, or sigil, of the crescent Moon:

If done in the daylight, anoint with the sigil of the Sun:

Now say:

> I CONSECRATE THEE IN THE NAMES OF EPONA AND
>   CERNUNNOS!
> THOU ART PROTECTED AND SACRED IN THEIR SIGHT.

Envision at this moment a cocoon of light surrounding the animal that is either golden (for the Sun) or silver (for the Moon). The blessing is now complete.

## Closing of the circle

Once you have blessed all of your animals, pick up each of the circle stones as you move in a counterclockwise motion, beginning in the North. Using your left foot, erase the circle you have made on the ground and say:

> NO ONE WILL FIND
> THE SACRED SHRINE.
> NO PRIEST WILL TREAD
> THE SPELL I'VE THREAD.

## NOTES

1. Ward Rutherford, *Celtic Mythology* (New York: Sterling Publishing Co., 1990)

2. Rutherford, 82.

3. Barbara G. Walker, *The Women's Encyclopedia of Myths and Secrets* (San Francisco: Harper and Row, 1983)

4. Rutherford, 141.

5. Rutherford, 88.

6. See, for example, Rutherford, 141.

7. Janet and Stewart Farrar, *The Witches' God* (Custer, Washington: Phoenix Publishing, 1989)

8. Farrar, 97.

9. The "cern" in both names is thought to refer to "horns." Rutherford, 88.

10. Rutherford, 84, 88.

11. The daylight hours are sacred to Cernunnos and the nighttime is the world of Epona. The Sun is representative of the God and typically male forces in nature and the Moon is the symbol of the Goddess and female energies. Of course, these symbols are not always the same in every pagan system. This is the generally accepted symbology of traditional English Wicca, which emphasizes equal energy polarity in nature.

12. Be sure to use the Fire symbol when blessing with this element.

13. When blessing animals with Fire and Air, it is always safer for the animal if you use the corresponding tools (the athame for Fire and the bell for Air). Here are some precautions to keep from frightening your animals. While using the athame or double-edged knife for the element of Fire, point the tip of the blade at the animal and hold it no closer than one foot from its body. Send the powers of Fire from within you through the blade. Never touch a blade to any animal for any purpose. Proceed with extreme caution when using your athame around an animal. Harming an animal, intentionally or otherwise, carries grave karmic repercussions. Be careful!

    When using the bell to stand in for incense, be sure you ring it softly and away from the animal's ears. Let the reverberation of the sound gently seep into the psyche of the animal.

# *grimoire familiar*

H ere are a few enchantments you may want to try with your physical Familiar. Because each of these are works of creative (i.e., constructive) magic, they should all be performed during the waxing Moon or—for best magical advantage—at the Full Moon. Remember, to keep your enchantments effective, try to create them in the construction of your magic circle.

## FAMILIAR DIVINATION

### HERBAL INFLUENCES DIVINATION

Gather the following herbs:

| Herb | Planetary Influence |
|------|---------------------|
| Marigold | Sun |
| Willow leaves | Moon |
| Basil | Mars |
| Fennel | Mercury |
| Roses | Venus |
| Sage | Jupiter |
| Juniper | Saturn |

Place the herbs in small heaps within a 12-inch-diameter circle. Set the Familiar before the herbs and ask:

> WHICH SPHERE OF INFLUENCE AM I CURRENTLY UNDER?

or,

> WHICH SPHERE OF INFLUENCE WILL GOVERN MY AFFAIRS IN _____ (name of activity)?

Whichever herb the animal is drawn to first is the sphere that influences you at this time:

Sun         Men's mysteries, riches, wealth, truth

Moon        Women's mysteries, home and hearth, intuition, emotions, cycles

Mars        Power, energy, sex, passion, conquests, battles

Mercury     Communication, ideas, magical influence, learning

Venus       Love, beauty, compassion, relationships, friends, artistic ventures

Jupiter     Prosperity, expansion, business, gain, happiness, joviality

Saturn      Karma, past life energies at work, decisions, laws, endings

## HERBAL DIVINATION METHOD NO. 2
(for questions requiring a yes or no answer)

Gather together two small bundles of herbs: one of marigold and one of juniper (i.e., for the Sun and for Saturn, respectively). Place them across from each other at least 12 inches apart.

Ask the animal a yes or no question. If the animal picks the juniper, the answer is no; if it is yes, it will pick the marigold.

# FAMILIAR DIVINATION—COLOR

Use the same method as employed in the Herbal Influences Divination, but instead of herbs, use circles of colored construction paper:[1]

| Planet | Color |
|--------|-------|
| Sun | Gold |
| Moon | White or Silver |
| Mars | Red |
| Mercury | Yellow |
| Venus | Pink |
| Jupiter | Green |
| Saturn | Black |

# BIRD DIVINATION

Take some wild birdseed and spread it on the ground in a circle. With your finger, draw the sigil of the element which influences your question:

For matters of romance, emotions, cycles, endings, closure, the past, or any other matter governed by the Moon, draw the sigil of Water: ▽

For questions concerning money, stability, wealth, old age secrets, hidden matters, or women's mysteries, draw the sigil of Earth: ▽

When asking about intelligence, education, communication, higher thought, births, new projects, or the future, draw the sigil of Air: △

If you have a question regarding passion, energy, motivation, sex, aggression, outward achievement, activity, or men's mysteries, draw the sigil of Fire: △

After you draw the appropriate sigil, hold your hands outstretched over the seed and say:

BIRDS OF THE WOOD
CREATURES OF FLIGHT,

CARRY MY QUERY;
BRING IT TO LIGHT!

Allow the birds to eat the seed for a while. But don't let them eat it all just yet. While there are still some seeds left, look at the patterns they form on the ground. In these patterns will be your answer. For this process, allow your spontaneous nature to override any previously held notions of what certain shapes and patterns "should" mean. Allow your initial impressions of the shapes and patterns to evolve an answer.

**Sample Question and Answer**

Q: When should I begin looking for a new job?

Draw the sigil of air for this one, since Air governs beginnings. However, the sigil of Fire would do as well, since it is related to outward achievement.

A: In the scattered seed I see two patterns: a broken spiral and two crossed lines. My interpretation of this would be that I should begin looking now because it is going to be a long journey to the achievement of the goal (the spiral formation). However, I need to proceed with a balanced perspective, first taking into account all aspects of my life (the cross).

# FAMILIAR MAGIC

## LOVE SPELL

**Colors:** Green or blue to begin a relationship with a woman; red or yellow to begin a relationship with a man.

**Planetary influence:** Venus

**Collect these objects**

- A small rosebud (of the color most appropriate for your working)

- A small scroll of parchment (about 3" x 5")

- A pen with red ink

- A small length of red ribbon

On the parchment, write the name of the one you love with the red-inked pen. Fill in the blank spaces of the paper with sigils of love, such as hearts or sigils of the planets Mars and Venus.

Mars: ♂     Venus: ♀

Place the rosebud in the center of the parchment and begin to roll the parchment into a scroll. Tie the parchment to the collar of your Familiar with the red or pink ribbon (if it wears a collar—if not place it near where the Familiar sleeps), saying:

> LOVE ME MINE,
> LOVE BE THINE,
> BRING OUR HEARTS TO THUS ENTWINE!

Leave the scroll with the Familiar for three days. Then remove it from the presence of the animal. Burn parchment, ribbon, and rosebud in the fireplace or in a censer on a Friday night and chant as it burns:

> PASSION, FIRE, INNER BURNING,
> BRING THE ONE FOR WHOM I'M YEARNING.
> COME SOUTH!
> COME WEST!
> COME NORTH!
> COME EAST!
> COME RIDING BY MY SACRED BEAST!

Imagine the one you love being led to you by your Familiar. It is done!

## PROSPERITY SPELL

### Collect these objects

- A dollar bill

- Bowl of water

- Green thread

- Salt

- Incense

- A small piece of blank parchment paper

- Silver, gold, or green candles to work by

This spell takes place in two parts. The first part allows a release of the old patterns of lack in your life. The second part uses the Familiar to draw prosperity.

### Part One

On the parchment paper, write down your current needs that are yet unmet. Hold the inscribed parchment over the burning incense, saying:

> THOU ART PURIFIED WITH THE POWER OF FIRE AND AIR.

Next, lay the parchment on the table and pour salt, the element of Earth, over it. Be sure to cover all of the words with the salt. Imagine the salt absorbing the situation that has been written down. Hold your hands over the parchment and say:

> THOU ART CLEANSED WITH THE POWER OF EARTH.

Take the parchment paper and allow the salt to slide off into the bowl of water. Stir the salt into the water, imagining that the old negative ways are dissolving with the salt. As you stir, say:

POWER OF WATER,
EARTH'S DAUGHTER,
PREPARE FOR ME
PROSPERITY.

Burn the parchment paper and imagine any remains of the negative situation burning to ashes. Mix the ashes with the water and salt. Dig a hole in the earth and pour the mixture into it, cover it over, and forget it. It is now neutralized.

**Part Two**

Now hold the dollar bill between your clasped hands, using your imagination to see the desired end. When you have a strong mental image, rub the dollar bill against the Familiar, saying:

ABUNDANCE BE MINE BY THE GODS' OWN LAW,
COME BY TALON OR HOOF, BY PAW OR CLAW!

Roll the money up and tie it with the green thread. Place it where it can lie undisturbed. The magical deed is done.

## HEALING MAGIC

This is a good way to heal yourself or another, providing you can bring the Familiar into the presence of the patient.

**What you'll need**

- Salt

- Water

- A small branch or twig in leaf of at least five inches in length (it can be from any kind of tree, but eucalyptus is especially good).

- A white, red, or green candle

- A sharp knife

Carve into the candle the name of the person to be healed along with one word describing the sick person's physical, mental or emotional problem. Purify the candle with salt and water while imagining the patient well again.

Next take the leafy branch and brush it against the patient (or a picture of the patient) in long, downward strokes. Begin at the head or chest and brush all the way down to the toes and even off the body completely. Imagine at this time that you are clearing away the negative influences that cloud the sick person's life at this time.

After this, anoint the person's head and the soles of the feet with salt and water.

Now bring around the Familiar and allow the patient to hold it. Whisper into your Familiar's ear the desired recovery. Then say aloud to the animal:

> BE OBEDIENT! HEAR MY WORD!
> BRING HEALTH WITH SPEED OF WINGED BIRD!

Light the candle and allow it to burn by the person's bedside until it burns all the way down.

## HOME OR BUSINESS PROTECTION

**Collect these items**
- A white or gold candle
- Blessing oil
- The Fire symbol: △

Move clockwise through each room starting at the front door. Lead your Familiar into each room of the home or office you want protected. End once again at the front door.

Stand at the entrance to each room and point the Fire symbol toward the center of the room. Call upon the power of your Familiar, saying:

> PROTECT ME AND MY (home/business) _____
> (magical name). BE THOU A GUARDIAN OF THIS PLACE.

After you announce this in each room, take a dab of blessing oil and anoint each doorway with the following protective symbol:

Once you arrive back at the front door, open it up and set the Familiar on the threshold, saying:

> BE THOU GONE, SPIRITS OF WICKEDNESS!
> BE THOU GONE, SPIRITS OF POVERTY AND DEARTH!
> BE THOU GONE, SPIRITS OF SICKNESS!
> THIS SPACE IS PROTECTED BY THE POWER OF
> _____ (familiar's name), A GUARDIAN
> BEAST OF EPONA AND CERNUNNOS!

While you are in the doorway, light the white candle and set it in a holder on the threshold for a moment or two. Anoint the doorway with oil, close the door and allow the candle to burn down near the door.

## PERSONAL PROTECTION

**What you'll need**
- Blessing oil

Turn your Familiar to face the East, saying:

> _____ (Familiar's name), BY THE POWER OF
> THE RISING SUN, MOON, AND STARS—PROTECT ME.

Turn the animal to the South, saying:

> _____ (Familiar's name), BY THE POWER OF
> DANCING FLAMES AND BY THY WARMTH—PROTECT ME.

Turn it to the West, saying:

_____ (Familiar's name), BY THE POWER OF THE SETTING SUN AND ALL THE MYSTERIES OF THE DEEP—PROTECT ME.

Finally, turn your Familiar to the North, saying:

_____ (FAMILIAR'S NAME), BY THE POWER OF YOUR SILENCE AND STRENGTH, BY THE POWER OF THE PLACE OF YOUR RETURN—PROTECT ME.

At the end of the enchantment, place a dab of blessing oil on your forehead. Visualize a white and gold light surrounding and protecting you and your Familiar.

## A FUR CHARM

### What you'll need
- Fur or hair from your Familiar
- A small charm bag (made of any material)

On the three nights of the Full Moon, take a grooming brush and smooth through your Familiar's fur. As you do this, begin to think about the blessings you may be needing in your life: inner peace, love, creativity, etc. With each brushstroke, say your desires out loud. As you work at this for several minutes, fur will accumulate in the bristles. Remove it from the brush and hold it between your hands, saying:

GENTLE BE THY WAYS,
EVEN BE THY PATH
AND EASY BE THY DAYS.
BRING TO ME MY HEART'S DESIRE
BY WATER, ROCK, WIND, AND FIRE!

Repeat this on each of the three Full Moon nights. Finally, place the fur you've collected into your charm bag and wear it to bring good fortune.

## NOTE

1. It doesn't matter whether or not your animal is color blind. You are the principal operator of the divination. Through you all of the universal energies collect. It is through the animal that they take focus and become manifest in an answer.

# *epilogue*

The modern Craft of the Wise is a living tradition. It is alive and vital because the imagery and symbolism it uses are applicable to the modern world and contemporary life. What makes Witchcraft's symbol system accessible is the fact that it is not bound in by literal interpretation. All of the Craft's deities, celebrations, and principles are concrete; they provide practical values, ethics, and a coherent philosophical structure. But at the same time, the meaning behind the symbols of our deities, celebrations, and principles comprises the living core of the craft. In other words, the forms of our symbols are never favored over their underlying import.

For Witches, the Goddess and God are as real as our own bodies, but at the same time we recognize the archetypes, the spiritual energies, which go far beyond physical forms. We also find the sacred in the physical elements: the air, fire, water, and earth. They are sacred not only because they sustain our physical lives, but because as symbols, they sustain our inward lives. Air is the symbol of knowledge and understanding; Fire symbolizes our passion, energy, and movement; our emotions are symbolized by Water; and our wisdom is well as our silences are embodied in the symbol of Earth.

However, Witchcraft and the many other Earth-based spiritual systems that embrace such constructs are not the norm in the West. Typically, Western religious systems focus on the outward forms of spirituality. Within a form-conscious mode, a system's followers must be led to "the truth" by another person; the faithful are taught to devalue their own inner voice. A natural outgrowth of this perspective is a secularized society that insists on finding a quantifiable value for everything, including spirituality; if something cannot be weighed, measured, or used to one's advantage, then it is to be disregarded. Individuals who focus in such an unbalanced way on the outward forms of any spiritual system are destined to feel unfulfilled.

A religion that fails to fulfill is on its way to dying out, and the final symptom of its death is that its adherents begin to experience alienation from its symbols, its ceremonies, and its Gods. Its mythology becomes a petrifact; it becomes dried up and useless, because the symbols are being translated as fact—as history, geography, or science. In many cases, nothing but the shell of outward form remains of the symbols, and religious life comes to the point of being nothing more than "going through the motions." The followers caught in such systems are subjected to shame and guilt for not feeling the deep connection they sense should be a part of journeying along a spiritual path.

Westerners are in crisis over their spiritual values, but crises move individuals into action and eventually it is individuals in action who effect change. Slowly, a shift in consciousness is taking place in the West. We are beginning to care for our planet. We are becoming more concerned with the interconnectedness of life as we recognize that the "value" of plants, animals, and our own lives is inherent, rather than a quantifiable commodity. A reverence for the natural world and, consequently, an altered view of deity is beginning to emerge from this paradigm shift.

The mainstream view of deity that has prevailed for centuries is that God is a being who claims to be the beginning and the end. He in essence says he's "it" and that nothing surpasses him. Layered on top of this model of God has been an emphasis on the outward, form-conscious, literal interpretation of symbols. The root of the consciousness from which this kind of system springs is one which affirms that God is separate and distinct from humans, plants, elements—and animals.

However, as we move in the direction of holistic consciousness and begin seeing the natural world not as something separate, but as a living extension of ourselves, a change takes place. No longer can we ignore the fact that the Earth sustains our lives, and that by abusing our resources we are actually cutting off our own life source. Operating within this new framework, the natural world becomes as valuable as our own lives; in essence, it becomes sacred and magical. In this emerging paradigm, the Earth and all Her creatures become a manifestation of the divine, rather than some foreign, lifeless object.

Where the Craft succeeds is in its ability to view deity in this liberated model, in which all of life is a divine manifestation. Rather than "worshipping" a God whose existence is independent from ours, the craft's mythology encourages an identification with the divine principle. The Gods of the Witches are not figments of imagination sitting on some distant cloud; rather, they pervade all that exists, seen and unseen. By working with nature and learning from Her, Witches participate in their deity because the Gods manifest through the very forces of life itself: in wind, water, stone, fire, and in all living creatures.

The Witch's identification with the animal power, the Familiar, is the extension of this principle. To the Witch, the Familiar is more than just the physical animal; it represents a power born of the unconscious. It is one of the many aspects of a living deity's expression. By identifying with the principle, the symbol, the energy, we participate in the perpetual renewal of our symbol system, which is the essence and life force of the Witch's Craft.

Wicca, shamanism, and other Earth-magic practices, although far from ever becoming mainstream spiritual systems, are at the fore of the West's change of consciousness. Practices such as working with the animal powers are a potent influence, helping to shape these new consciousness constructs.

The Familiar Self, reclaimed as a tool of self empowerment and transformation, challenges each of us to assume one of the traditional roles of the Witch. Once empowered by the inner Familiar, Witches effectively become the boon bringers of a community; they become the teachers, counselors, midwives, healers, priestesses, and priests.

As teachers and counselors, the Familiar Self calls us to guide other people who are ready to make the transition to a holistic mode of life. Teachers and counselors are spiritually empowered to model an interconnectedness of their personal life to the lives of others and to the rest of the natural world.

As midwives, healers, priestesses, and priests, Witches are called by the inner Familiar to assist in the rebirth of spirit. Those who assume these roles are empowered to make the wisdom of traditional teachings accessible. They apply a healing potion to the near fatal wounds of an ailing community by speaking in simple truths, by finding spirit in all that exists, and by pointing to common links in an otherwise diverse society.

Through this work, our role of Witch-as-magician becomes manifest. As magical folk, we firmly establish a collective identity as a spiritual community intent on practicing the axiom of changing consciousness—not only for ourselves, but for the planet—by working with the Familiar Self.

# *animal powers list*

**B**elow is a list of Familiar animals. In this list I include three categories to guide your consideration of each animal. The **Key Words** are usually two or three words that sum up the essence of the animal energy as lent to your personality. The **Personality** category details the personality traits of individuals who have these animals as Familiar selves. The **Magical Influences** are the abilities that each of these animal powers adds to your life.

A good practice for Familiar work is to keep a journal of any additional magical influences each animal adds to your spiritual work. If you'd like to share your experiences with me, I'd be more than happy to receive your input. With your help, this glossary of animals and their powers can expand.

## AARDVARK

**Key Words**—Powerful, secretive, justice-oriented

**Magical Influences**—Home protection, allows justice to prevail

**Personality**—Aardvarks pursue uncommon goals and paths. They shy away from danger by finding ways to hide. They do not like to have the home environment disturbed and will go to great lengths to see that all remains in status quo. This is a very Earthy animal; in fact, aardvark means "earth pig" in Afrikaans.

## ALLIGATOR

**Key Words**—Watchful, guarded

**Magical Influences**—Longevity, immortality

**Personality**—Alligators are literally tough-skinned animals. They can be impervious to the comments and influences of others, keeping their eyes on a single goal. Alligators are sluggish, and often live to be incredibly old. They are also devoted to their homes, although these may very well be hovels. To invoke alligator power is to invoke the powers of immortality.

## ANTEATER

**Key Words**—Seeking, unwavering, probing

**Magical Influences**—Diligence, determination, guardian of lost objects (can aid you in finding them)

**Personality**—Anteaters will generally have a wry or offbeat sense of humor. They can be avid readers and particularly enjoy solving a good mystery. They are natural analysts. Anteater personalities are good researchers, are usually business-minded, and keep their "noses to the grindstone."

## ANTELOPE

**Key Words**—Swift, flighty, high-strung, ultrasensitive

**Magical Influences**—Guardian of journeys, swift flows of high physical energy, foresight

**Personality**—The antelope loves groups, but don't expect someone who aligns with this power to hang around the party too long. Antelopes live on the move. The person aligning with Antelope has a naturally higher sense of intuition and can sense danger long before it ever arrives.

## ARMADILLO

**Key Words**—Protective, watchful, purposeful

**Magical Influences**—Protection of others, discovering secrets, determination

**Personality**—This is a feisty but slow-moving animal. Those who naturally align with this power would be proficient in battle when push comes to shove, but generally they stay out of the way of others.

## BABOON

**Key Words**—Family-oriented, protective

**Magical Influences**—Family protection, extensions of personal family, enlarging circle of friends, creating support network

**Personality**—Baboons show concern for whomever they consider to be family. Family does not necessarily mean blood relations; they take into the fold any individual considered worthy of attention. Baboons strongly defend their loved ones.

## BADGER

**Key Words**—Strong, watchful, hard-working, volatile

**Magical Influences**—Analytical ability, expansion of conscious mind abilities, mental alertness

**Personality**—The badger wants no more than to mind its own business. It doesn't understand when others don't do the same. It is serious-minded, but can have a quick and biting wit. When the badger is angry, he or she bristles the fur to look more than twice the normal size, as well as baring huge fangs. In actuality, badgers are berry eaters; the teeth are just for show. They use illusion of threats to keep enemies at bay. The badger is an excellent worker and can sometimes verge on workaholism.

## BAT

**Key Words**—Overtly sexual, worrier, self-determined

**Magical Influences**—Clairaudience, psychic sensitivity, sex; creates lust in the hearts of others

**Personality**—Bats are highly sexual in their personal dealings. Conversation can be laced with ribaldry. They are natural business persons. Since one of their governing heavenly bodies is the Moon, they can have drastic mood swings in their everyday life—one minute happy-go-lucky, the next irritable.

## BEAR

**Key Words**—Nurturing, loving, maternal, strong-willed

**Magical Influences**—Promotes healing, motherly love, guardian of emotional strength and mental stability

**Personality**—Bears can't help but intimidate others who may not know them, but the truth is that they can be very nurturing, open-hearted, and playful. Bears are highly intelligent and their curiosity is easily piqued. A bear always knows what everyone's weaknesses are and will strike in the soft underbelly if threatened.

## BEAVER

**Key Words**—Constructive, fun-loving, carefree, observant

**Magical Influences**—Prosperity, creative ability, the healing of relationships

**Personality**—Beaver types never want to be tied down to anything, except in one area of their lives—relationships. Beavers mate for life. They are also among the most creative of the animal personality types. They are constructive and try to stay focused with personal projects.

## BISON

**Key Words**—Practical, steadfast, affectionate, stubborn

**Magical Influences**—Patience, ability to manifest the desires of the self or others, mastery of the element of Earth

**Personality**—To the rest of the world, the bison looks as sturdy as an oak tree—firmly rooted in practical matters. This type works actively to create this appearance. The bison can be extremely opinionated and "bull headed." Bisons strive for a sense of security in their personal world. The bison can also be a natural psychic or mystic, but must get out of stubbornness to develop these talents.

## BOAR

**Key Words**—Direct, aggressive, enterprising

**Magical Influences**—Courage, reveals one's true life purpose

**Personality**—Although boars can be quick-tempered, they are one of the most energetic and enthusiastic personality types. Boars may find it difficult to be patient with situations or people they dislike. But they are quick-witted and have a knack for bringing humor into everyday events.

## BOBCAT

**Key Words**—Powerfully emotional, subtle

**Magical Influences**—Heightened perception of immediate surroundings, power to make the right choice

**Personality**—Added to the basic nature of the cat is a sense of wildness. The bobcat is more alert than an ordinary house cat. On the other hand, bobcats like to have a routine—more so than house cats. They have surprising strength for their usually small stature.

## BULL

**Key Words**—Sexual, strong-willed, trustworthy

**Magical Influences**—Male sexual energy is stressed here. The powers of sexual potency and pleasure are aroused. Fertility. Simplification of mundane matters. Evokes the Horned God and His power

**Personality**—Contrary to what you may first think, men are not the only ones who align with bull energy. Male and female bull qualities can be expressed through a healthy sexual appetite, by strength in business sense, by a good head for financial matters, or by yang energies in general. The main focus of bull personalities throughout the course of their lives is good food, good sex, and a beautiful place to live.

## BUZZARD

**Key Words**—Open, ingenious, crafty

**Magical Influences**—Subconscious mind, mental alertness, psychic awareness

**Personality**—Buzzards find thermals—air pockets—which they use to hold them aloft for hours without their ever having to flap their giant wings. Similarly, buzzard types are generally well-meaning, but they have a tendency to look for easy ways around tough tasks. This can be useful for an inventor who is trying to develop easier ways to approach certain tasks. Unchecked, however, buzzards can become a bit lazy. They are usually optimistic and can see "the big picture" easier than others.

## CAMEL

**Key Words**—Stable, sensitive, loving, enduring maternal care

**Magical Influences**—Endurance, stability in mundane matters, meditation

**Personality**—Camels are shrewd and can deal with adverse conditions without much stress. Their internal stores of "water" (actually fat deposits), the feminine principle, gives them an emotionally sensitive quality. Camels are good at making relationships work in the long run by finding the rough spots and smoothing them over. Camels make good counselors, and like to help others who find it difficult to weather the personal storms of life.

## CAT

 **Key Words**—Mysterious, independent, intellectual, inventive

**Magical Influences**—Magical visions, independence, strengthens one's magical potency, ability to move between the worlds with ease

**Personality**—The cat personality carries over into the entire cat family—lions, tigers, cougars, etc. So apply the powers and personality traits listed here to the entire feline family. The cat personality is highly independent. Cats have ways of getting what they want, one way or another. They won't often think of how their actions affect others, but they generally don't intend malice. Cats are born mysterious and can evoke spiritual aid without much trouble. They are trickster-teachers who might just take a swipe at others in order to teach a lesson. They can revert to being wild creatures without much notice.

## CHEETAH

**Key Words**—Affable, quick-witted, independent

**Magical Influences**—Physical speed, mastery of the element of Fire, ability to claim any desire

**Personality**—Cheetahs are great at tracking down their prey. This makes them great at achieving goals most would consider "long-shots." They are so quick-witted that they can insult someone without the insulted party ever taking notice. Cheetahs can be impatient and they can strive for lesser goals if they don't have a grasp of their true potential. They can be clinging in romantic situations and will "attack" their partner if they ever try to end things.

## CHIMPANZEE

**Key Words**—Intelligence, honesty, inquisitiveness

**Magical Influences**—Humor, intellectual development, produces probing questions about any given subject, evokes honesty in others

**Personality**—Chimpanzees are wonderfully gifted beings. They are natural teachers, but want us to learn from experience. Chimps are boisterous at times with their humor, but they will never forsake a friend in need. Chimpanzees are quality players. If you need to "lighten up," this is one of the better essences to evoke.

## CHINCHILLA

**Key Words**—Warm, optimistic

**Magical Influences**—Female sexuality is emphasized here. Love, tenderness, ability to attract a mate; also financial stability

**Personality**—Animal behaviorists would never deny that the chinchilla is a highly sexual animal. Those who have this personality will spend a great deal of time and energy focusing on sex. However, the chinchilla personality also knows the secrets of drawing creature comforts into his or her life. Chinchilla types can become easily lost in the illusion of materiality. They begin to adopt the attitude, "Why not? You only live once. How could this be bad for me?" They need to spend time each day affirming their spirituality, or reaching out to others.

## CHIPMUNK

**Key Words**—Realistic, conservative, hard-working

**Magical Influences**—Material comfort, money, prosperity

**Personality**—Chipmunks can be very spry. They usually have bubbly personalities which hide a secret self. This other side of their personality can manifest itself in a spendthrift attitude, or, conversely, in a severe work ethic. Nevertheless, chipmunks definitely know how to save and acquire money and luxury. They need to spend time each day doing relaxation exercises.

## CONDOR

**Key Words**—Wise, visionary, sage-like

**Magical Influences**—Foresight, wisdom, counseling ability

**Personality**—Condors are wise souls. They can see through the thickest hide of a personality right down to the bare soul. They intuitively know what makes any given person tick. They are born to counsel others with techniques that integrate body, mind, and spirit. They are truly heralds of the Aquarian Age. They are also visionaries and can see the true potential of others.

## COUGAR

**Key Words**—Stealthy, silent, capricious

**Magical Influences**—Broadening the subconscious mind, ability to keep secrets, healing through purification, physical strength

**Personality**—Adding to the cat's basic nature, we find in the cougar a sense of unlimited creativity. Writers, poets, musicians, actors, and artists often have cougar personalities. They are born showpersons, with an internal gauge of when to use their persuasive charm. Cougars heal others through mystical means, and some can even aspire to positions in the healing arts.

## COW

**Key Words**—Solid, nurturing, Goddess energy

**Magical Influences**—Solidification of matters, nurturing, prophetic dreams

**Personality**—The cow is sacred to many Goddesses, and as such the cow personality is graced with the powers of the Goddess—nurturing, compassion, and inner wisdom. The cow personality turns inward, focusing on matters of the spirit or on helping and nurturing others. The cow's magical qualities manifest whatever it needs, but on a slow, methodical, natural basis. The cow type loves children and can easily go into teaching as a career.

## COYOTE

**Key Words**—Versatile, persevering, clever

**Magical Influences**—Adaptability, wins the favor of the Lady of the Moon, magically changes other's opinions, draws down Moon power

**Personality**—Coyotes are true loners; they are wary of strangers and usually have a better time alone than with another person. But coyotes mate for life and they make long-lasting companions for those who get close enough. Coyotes are "jacks-of-all-trades"; they are able to survive all odds because of their adaptability. Eventually they try to master internal and magical power.

## CROW

**Key Words**—Communicative, feisty, manipulative

**Magical Influences**—Magical prowess, self-control, creation of illusion

**Personality**—Crows are manipulators. They are like chess players who make all the people in their lives their chess pieces. Either verbally, emotionally, or magically, they tend to get what they want through the manipulation of others. Crows are territorial and will fight for what they feel is, by rights, theirs. Crows hate to give up the ghost, so they can be extremely determined in whatever matters they set their minds to. Most crows like to have plenty of time to themselves and can appear to be loners.

## DEER

**Key Words**—Shy, light, sensitive, intuitive

**Magical Influences**—Peace, tranquility, easing of nerves, ability to see future events clearly

**Personality**—Deer are true introverts; they shy away from any suspected confrontation. They know who their enemies are and steer clear of them. Deer are among the most psychically sensitive personality types; they can impart information about events moments before they happen. They are quite at peace with themselves and the world.

## DINGO

**Key Words**—Strong-witted, stealthy, sneaky

**Magical Influences**—Invisibility, stealth

**Personality**—The dingo personality is less open and apparent than the dog's. The dingo is secretive, manipulative, and sometimes opportunistic. These are not necessarily negative traits, however; for example, they can be channeled into a business savvy like no other. The dingo can come and go unnoticed, so this personality type needs to really raise a ruckus in order to get some attention. Dingos can be introverts.

## DINOSAUR

**Key Words**—Transcendent, aggressive, unsentimental

**Magical Influences**—Breaking through to new levels, diminishing sentimentality in the self or in others, self-transformation on many levels

**Personality**—Dinosaurs can be aggressive in their dealings, but they possess the unique ability to change their circumstances dramatically. They know when changes are needed, and do not hesitate to make them.

## DOG

**Key Words**—Humanitarian, understanding, unconditionally loving

**Magical Influences**—Lasting friendships, optimism, happiness, a true world-consciousness, love

**Personality**—Dogs are diggers and hunters by nature. They have the ability to find anything (this is useful in recovering lost items). Dogs are friendly to most people and try to find the good in every event in their lives. They can be good religious figures because of their non-condemning nature. They also hold strong ties to their parental figures and often live with the parents well into adulthood.

## DOLPHIN

**Key Words**—Sociable, articulate, progressive, scientific, detached

**Magical Influences**—Increase of intelligence, clarity of speech, peace for the self and for others

**Personality**—Dolphins are naturally curious beings. They want to be fair in their dealings and actually go out of their way to find balance. Since they are quite social, they depend on the company of others to make them feel complete. They usually either come from or create large, extended families.

## DONKEY

**Key Words**—Hard working, conscientious, die-hard

**Magical Influences**—Memory, stopping grief or depression, ability to resolve the Karma of this lifetime

**Personality**—The donkey is a workaholic, but he or she has a very sharp sense of humor. This is the type who can say startling things to throw you off balance without looking at all unnerved. Donkeys can be shy, but once they get to know everyone, they can be the life of the party. They can often have a loud, distinctive laugh. They are optimists who consciously try not to fall into negative thinking.

## DOVE

**Key Words**—Peaceful, loving, spiritually idealistic

**Magical Influences**—Physical beauty, love, spirituality, reveals one's spiritual mission

**Personality**—In the traditional sense, the dove stands for peace and love. Doves are harbingers of gentility and of high spiritual ideals. They are messengers of spirit and can be spiritual teachers. Doves have some trouble, though, finding their personal equilibrium and stability.

## DRAGON

**Key Words**—Powerful, grand, wise

**Magical Influences**—Magical adeptness, mastery of self-control, reveals the hidden knowledge of ancient mysteries, evokes aid of salamanders, mastery of the element of Fire

**Personality**—The dragon is a very wise being. Usually, the person with the dragon personality seems like an "old soul," capable of inspiring those who are seekers of higher truth. The dragon guards its jewels of wisdom jealously, giving them only to those who prove themselves worthy.

## DUCK—See MALLARD

## EAGLE

**Key Words**—Powerful, thoughtful, intense

**Magical Influences**—Spirit flight (astral projection), acute vision, monogamy, attainment of high aspirations; mastery of the element of Air, evokes aid of sylphs

**Personality**—Eagles are commanding presences. Whether they want to or not, they attract attention. Those with this animal personality have strong leadership skills and take swift action when it is needed. They also tend to mate for life and cannot understand how others can be happy with relationships that are anything but monogamous.

## ELEPHANT

**Key Words**—Justice-oriented, people-loving, dominant

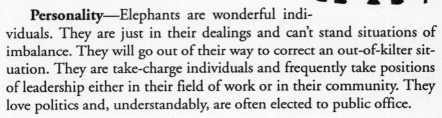

**Magical Influences**—Longevity, memory enhancement, restful sleep, imperviousness

**Personality**—Elephants are wonderful individuals. They are just in their dealings and can't stand situations of imbalance. They will go out of their way to correct an out-of-kilter situation. They are take-charge individuals and frequently take positions of leadership either in their field of work or in their community. They love politics and, understandably, are often elected to public office.

## FALCON

**Key Words**—Solitary, independent, driven

**Magical Influences**—Brings desired solitude, heightens sense of independence (cuts dependency cycles), ability to win favors

**Personality**—Falcons are loners by nature. They seem to enjoy life best when left alone. Since the falcons stay to themselves, they have few or no enemies. When the falcon makes a friend, he or she becomes extremely protective and loyal. Falcons are great hunters and enjoy all games of skill.

## FERRET

**Key Words**—Fun-loving, playful, optimistic, curious

**Magical Influences**—True happiness, joy, lightens up heavy moods

**Personality**—Those who identify with the ferret are sure to be outgoing individuals. They are generally happy-go-lucky, spontaneous, and inventive. Ferrets are playful creatures, but like to stir things up—much to the distress of others. They can be practical jokers. Ferrets are good at finding things out and investigating areas of interest. Because of their usually pleasant disposition, they are popular and can assume leadership positions.

## FLAMINGO

**Key Words**—Choosy, enlightened, balanced

**Magical Influences**—Ability to sort things out, peace, inner balance

**Personality**—In the wild, flamingos spend most of their day filtering algae-filled waters through their beaks. This makes them quite analytical and able to sort out the good or useful elements in their life from the bad or useless ones. They are peaceful, gentle, balance-oriented creatures.

## FOX

**Key Words**—Stealthy, charming, analytical

**Magical Influences**—Ingenuity, cunning, the ability to charm others, teaching ability, powers with herbs

**Personality**—The fox is a trickster-teacher and enjoys stirring up trouble so those involved can learn from the experience. They have the ability to charm people; however, they may use this to lure their enemies and then go in for the attack. Foxes are highly intuitive.

## FROG

**Key Words**—Flexible, adaptable, balanced

**Magical Influences**—Brings forth change, articulation of emotional issues, power to drive others with words

**Personality**—The frog personality is one that seeks and enjoys change. Frogs have a good natural balance between the conscious and unconscious minds. They are articulate individuals and they love any chance to speak their mind. They can be persuasive beings who can change the minds of others.

# GAZELLE

**Key Words**—Watchful, group-oriented, internally alive

**Magical Influences**—Protection from enemies, overcoming obstacles

**Personality**—Gazelles are people-loving individuals. They function best in partnerships, families, groups and communities. They tend to hold back from expressing their fullest potential, preferring instead to fall back on the power and influence of the group. Once they find what they are good at, they can be leaders in their chosen fields.

# GIRAFFE

**Key Words**—Casual, friendly

**Magical Influences**—Ability to endure long periods without sleep. Guardian of long-lasting friendships, relaxation

**Personality**—Giraffes are laid-back types. They are never uptight when they make a mistake; they just move right along. Since they don't stress out much, their bodies don't create enough toxins to make them sleep for long periods of time. The giraffe is the symbol of friendship for many of the tribal folk of Africa.

# GOAT

**Key Words**—Impervious, wandering, steadfast

**Magical Influences**—Guards against food poisoning, clears away old and unwanted situations from one's life

**Personality**—Goats usually are task-oriented creatures. They prefer to concentrate on the job at hand rather than coordinating multiple chores. One problem with this is that goat types tend to concentrate on one area for so long that they "burn out" and can no longer generate interest for themselves in that subject.

# GORILLA

**Key Words**—Strong, expansive, orderly

**Magical Influences**—Structure, release from tension

**Personality**—Gorilla types love order and structure in their lives. They can make good military officers, bookkeepers, and sports coaches. One problem is that they have trouble recognizing the personal boundaries of others; they tend to take over situations they feel need more discipline without asking permission.

# HARE

**Key Words**—Independent, solitary, skittish

**Magical Abilities**—Heightening of physical senses, mastery of Moon magic, helps women in channeling the Moon Goddess and connecting with the Eleusinian Mysteries

**Personality**—Hares are quite versatile beings. They are not as gentle and docile as one might imagine. Hares avoid danger by lying low. That, however, is their entire life-tactic. They can be evasive in their speaking patterns. When they become interested in a mate, they tend to show off and put forward a face that is not really indicative of their true nature. They can make good politicians.

# HIPPOPOTAMUS

**Key Words**—Matriarchal, balanced

**Magical Influences**—Teaching ability, ability to understand more than one perspective

**Personality**—Those who have the hippo personality are drawn to strong female figures and often form unbreakable attachments with more than one woman (mother, a sister, a lover, or just a friend). They prefer careers in which they can work with or express emotion. Children of hippo types are intelligent because of the deliberate teaching and attention they receive.

# HORSE

**Key Words**—Wild, expressive, stately

**Magical Influences**—Ability to gain the help of individuals or communities, regain of one's lost spirit, soul recovery. Ability to return to a natural, wild state

**Personality**—The horse personality cannot bear to be tied down to any person, place, or situation. If they are tied down, they cannot help but rise to the top and be placed in command. They are leaders, but they really don't care if anyone follows. They have the ability to rouse the general public into action, as they naturally have their fingers on the pulse of the populace.

## HYENA

**Key Words**—Androgynous and mystical

**Magical Influences**—Ability to find the magical name of any object or person

**Personality**—Hyenas are complex. They choose not to conform to society's expectations; they feel compelled to break free of political/social sexual stereotypes. They have a natural connection with the planet Mercury and therefore have control over a great deal of magical energy.

## IGUANA

**Key Words**—Tricky, moody, changeable

**Magical Influences**—Quickening of reflexes, dexterity, control of the weather

**Personality**—Iguanas prefer to choose paths that others would not dare to tread. They like to have company on their nontraditional roads. No one controls an iguana for very long. They have greatly developed senses, but this tends to make them hyper-vigilant and high-strung.

## JACKAL

**Key Words**—Family loving, extroverted

**Magical Influences**—Finding lost articles, strengthening, and healing the bond with parents, ability to change present circumstances, turns enemies into friends

**Personality**—Not many will claim the jackal as a Familiar Self because it has so often been used as a term of contempt. However, the jackal is a strongly positive personality type. It prefers to work in group settings and is efficient in getting any work done that is set before it. Jackals have strong attachments to their parents or those who are parental figures in their lives.

## JAGUAR

**Key Words**—Mysterious, self-preserving

**Magical Influences**—Revelation of secrets and mysteries, self-protection

**Personality**—The jaguar must feel as though it is the king or queen of its domain, whether at home, work, or play. Jaguars feel as though most people owe them something at some level and are always ready to collect. They can defend and protect an enemy from public humiliation simply to have the first chance at taking a swipe at him. They need to feel loved by all and cannot stand the idea that someone may find them intolerable.

## KANGAROO

**Key Words**—Ingenious, solid, earthy

**Magical Influences**—Ease in childbirth, spiritual rebirth

**Personality**—Kangaroos are born "twice"—once from the mother's womb and once from the pouch. This makes them masters at rebirthing and knowing the ways of rebirth. They prefer a balanced, earthy mental position, but also enjoy getting silly and going "out in left field" with friends. Kangaroos make good midwives, obstetricians, or psychologists because of their connection with birth and rebirth energy.

## KOALA

**Key Words**—Laid back, passive, positive

**Magical Influences**—Temporary infertility, protects the home from fires, raises one's level of optimism

**Personality**—Koalas are people in their own world. They are sensitive and kind to others and avoid all kinds of danger simply by not believing in it. This trait can go a bit overboard and lead to naivete and indulgence in unrealistically optimistic fantasies. They enjoy the fine arts and can be artists or singers themselves.

## LEOPARD

**Key Words**—Shy, wary, active

**Magical Influences**—Power to claim karmic rewards from the universe, ability to hide

**Personality**—Leopards do not like to be in the spotlight. In work they tend to take on behind-the-scenes tasks. Even though they remain in the background, they can be powerfully influential forces in the lives of others. They are extremely self-directed and set realistic, obtainable goals. They would prefer to achieve their goals without the aid of others, but they know the value of a cooperative effort.

## LION

**Key Words**—Wise, broadminded, honest

**Magical Influences**—Evokes power of the Sun, helps men in channeling the Sun God, generosity, enthusiasm, wisdom, honesty

**Personality**—Lions are magnanimous and creative individuals. They tend to put themselves into situations that broaden their horizons. They can be broadminded and open to variations in the culture and lifestyle of others. They are natural leaders and organizers. Sometimes they need to keep a pompous attitude under control.

## MALLARD

**Key Words**—Friendly, compassionate, emotional

**Magical Influences**—Friendship, meditation, balances the four elements within the self

**Personality**—Ducks are creatures of habit. They can go through life on automatic pilot if they are not careful. An example is how mallards migrate at certain times of the year. Duck people can feel at home almost anywhere, and generally make whatever space they occupy their home away from home. Ducks like to teach others and can generally do so through humor and wit.

## MINK

**Key Words**—Inquisitive, conservative, changeable

**Magical Influences**—Avoidance of or escape from dangerous situations

**Personality**—Minks are lively and talkative individuals. They tend to change their minds often and are easily influenced by the thoughts of others. Minks tend to be a bit on the skittish or nervous side. They work hard for their money and know how to spend and save wisely. This can sometimes border on miserliness, however.

## MOOSE

**Key Words**—Community-oriented, graceful, hospitable

**Magical Influences**—Power to shed the past; heightens one's social graces

**Personality**—The moose can live to be quite old. It will live and work in a community setting, but prefers to be alone with nature. As a result, the moose occasionally disappears from its usual haunts to spend time in the forests, mountains, or wilderness. It is maternally oriented, and you will never hear a moose complain about his or her mother. The moose is sensitive to the rudeness and crudeness of others and strives to appear cultured and polished.

## MOUSE

**Key Words**—Curious, fidgety

**Magical Influences**—Finding ways around obstacles, heightening one's hearing, ability to get beyond closed doors

**Personality**—Mice are not really all that extroverted. They detest surprises and shocks of any kind and prefer the comfort of routine. They are able to find ways of getting what they want, but they are silent and swift movers on the job. Once they find a living space they like, they can settle in for the rest of their lives. Mouse personalities communicate telepathically with other people, and with animals as well.

# ORANGUTAN

**Key Words**—Bright, cheerful, protective

**Magical Influences**—Guardian of trees; mastery of tree magic, evokes the aid of tree spirits

**Personality**—Orangutans will live and work in organized society, but prefer an anarchic approach. They are loyal to what few friends they open up to. They don't necessarily like to keep to themselves, but that is how they end up. They love to debate philosophical and theological points and can be proverbial "professional students," since they thirst for knowledge and truth throughout much of their lives. Once they find what is truth for them, they can be very protective of it and close their minds to further inquiry.

# OSTRICH

**Key Words**—Extremely wary, nonconformist, original

**Magical Influences**—Power to detect disturbances from long distances; heals digestive problems

**Personality**—The ostrich person can be very shy. It is also very wary of new people and situations. Ostriches prefer to observe, make their decisions, and then act on them. They are often nonconformists who live by their own set of rules, morals, and standards. However, they do not like others to know that they are nontraditional.

# OTTER

**Key Words**—Elusive, joyful, spritely

**Magical Influences**—Physical flexibility; ability to take the form of another, mastery of the element of Water, healing

**Personality**—Otter types like to be alone, but often enjoy the company of others. When they get together with friends, they are so adaptable that they mirror their company's behavior, language, and even thought patterns. If an otter is in the presence of some other strong personality for too long, it loses its sense of exactly who it is. Otters need to set goals for themselves because they can easily lose track of where they are going in life.

## OWL

**Key Words**—Stealthy, territorial, precise

**Magical Influences**—Spirituality, lunar healing, magical vision, ability to see spirits; can create closure, allows one to see past lives

**Personality**—Owls are usually industrious and intelligent. They are innately aligned with death and the mysteries surrounding death. They can become engrossed in this subject, but ultimately they affirm the positive life-after-death theme. Owls have few enemies, but when they attack, they strike with deadly accuracy. Owls need to have a place to call their own—even if it is just a corner of a room.

## PARROT

**Key Words**—Raucous, boisterous, silly

**Magical Influences**—Enhances the learning of foreign languages, ability to assume the voice of another, power to mimic

**Personality**—The parrot type is prone to indulge in fun-loving pranks. Parrots enjoy humor and never turn down the chance to pull off a good practical joke. They can manipulate their voices with ease, and this lends to their interest in foreign languages and vocal mimicry. Parrots can be easily hurt by others because they sometimes lack a solid, positive self-image.

## PIG

 **Key Words**—Noncommittal, freedom-loving, magical

**Magical Influences**—Channeling the Goddess, helps those who make promises to keep their word

**Personality**—Pigs are freedom-loving creatures. They don't want to feel obligated to others and will therefore avoid getting caught in long-term relationships and commitments. As a result they tend to have plenty of free time to work on themselves. They enjoy digging in the past and are attracted to anthropology and archaeology. They can be easily made to feel guilty, and once they start on that cycle it takes a long time before they are finished wallowing in self-pity. The Sow is the animal of the Crone.

## RABBIT

**Key Words**—Timid, introspective

**Magical Influences**—Enhances rapport with the Goddess and the God, makes one appear sage-like, meditation, knowledge

**Personality**—Rabbits are timid creatures. They don't care much for parties and lots of small talk. They live in their own little world where they feel safe and protected. They are naturally meditative, and for this reason they can be attracted to professional psychic counseling. In this trade, they prefer methods of divination that rely more on intuitive processes, rather than on mechanics.

## RACCOON

**Key Words**—Adaptable, sly, dexterous

**Magical Influences**—Physical or mental dexterity, skill with hands, makes one fastidious

**Personality**—Raccoons hate secrets; they want to know how and why everything works. They are friendly people who have no fears about approaching strangers for conversation. They often live for the moment and find time each day to celebrate life in their own way. Raccoons are tidy and modest but can also become overly fastidious. They can be fussy about the food they eat.

## RAT

**Key Words**—Home loving, perceptive

**Magical Influences**—Fertility, magical energy, ability to move through solid matter

**Personality**—Rats are territorial creatures. They emphasize their home environment and much of their lives (both in business and pleasure) revolves around the home. They also tend to desire a large family. They are very observant individuals. They can easily blend into their immediate environment.

## RAVEN

**Key Words**—Innocent, playful, joker

**Magical Influences**—Makes one a prankster, begins new ventures, success, power to make the right choices, reveals future lives

**Personality**—Animal equivalent of the Tarot trump card, The Fool. Ravens can be quite profound in their philosophical thinking, yet they present themselves in such an unassuming way that it is difficult for others to get the raven's message. They are life-affirming and prefer simplicity in all matters. They are problem solvers and can handle even the most difficult people with success.

## RHINOCEROS

**Key Words**—Petulant, reluctant, confined

**Magical Influences**—Sharpens sense of smell, aids one in setting down roots, lends the power to successfully fashion an aphrodisiac

**Personality**—The Rhinoceros is concerned with earthy subjects: good food, good sex, and a nice place to live. But rhinos also sense that the spiritual world eventually has power over the physical world, and this keeps them from overindulgence. They are at their physical and mental peak in the morning hours and by noon are ready to call it a day. They can be strongly attracted to members of the opposite sex. They can also be possessive of friends.

# SEAL

**Key Words**—Competitive, understanding

**Magical Influences**—Prosperity, expansion, power to overcome negative emotional cycles

**Personality**—The seal loves competition and faces it with relish. The seal personality can also be compassionate when he or she realizes that their competitor was never really up to the race. Seals are quite playful and intelligent beings. They can fathom the depths of heady philosophical challenges, and are often the movers and shakers in the field of philosophy.

# SKUNK

**Key Words**—Defensive, confident

**Magical Influences**—Protects against snake bites, stops gossip, ability to defend oneself without the infliction of physical harm

**Personality**—Those who identify with the skunk are usually unassuming and quiet. They are natural teachers and enjoy the company of children. They are often drawn to people who present themselves as wise or knowledgeable. They don't allow the insults of others to affect them.

# SQUIRREL

**Key Words**—Precise, exacting, clever

**Magical Influences**—Wisdom, perfect timing, creates beneficial coincidences

**Personality**—Squirrels love to be free. They are watchful of their home and personal belongings. Squirrels have the capacity to figure out how things work. Once a squirrel absorbs the information it needs, it then can take action—but not until it knows the ground rules does it feel comfortable.

# TIGER

**Key Words**—Powerful, resistant, strong

**Magical Influences**—Invokes the aid of the Huntress Goddess, Artemis; heightens hearing and physical strength, heals fevers

**Personality**—Tigers like anonymity and assume aliases in many endeavors. They prefer jobs in which they have little personal contact with the public. They tend to take up residence in areas with cooler climates. Tiger females are particularly interested in female issues and feminism in general. Tigers encourage strength in their partners and family members. They cannot understand (nor can they tolerate) weak-willed individuals.

## UNICORN

**Key Words**—Virginal, pure, airy

**Magical Influences**—Abstinence from sex, harmony with nature, resonance with the Goddess energies of the Maiden, good beginnings, personal magical power

**Personality**—Unicorns are quite elusive individuals. They have close relationships with very few people. They remain faithful to a lover over a lifetime. They live for romance and simple pleasures like strolling through gardens and smelling fragrant flowers. They are handy with Old-World-style crafts such as soap making and the weaving of fabric. Unicorns prefer the company of women.

## WALRUS

**Key Words**—Easy-going, sleepy, not easily provoked

**Magical Influences**—Fortifies teeth, protects children, balances those who are emotionally high-strung

**Personality**—Walruses find their strength and security from within. They know the value of a group effort and prefer to socialize in groups and clubs that have a loose organization. They are able to take the value of wisdom gained through the mistakes of others and apply it in their own lives. Walruses are resourceful. They can be a bit on the lazy side, but once in action they are unstoppable.

# WEASEL

**Key Words**—Ferocious, courageous, relentless

**Magical Influences**—Patron of warriors and those in battle, protects against nightmares and all evil forces

**Personality**—Weasels are fiery, feisty, energetic people. They love to fight for what is right and can single handedly take on corporations and large special interest groups—usually with success. They tend to worry about small things in their lives. Weasels are good at starting up new and original projects. They prefer innovation over routine and can be pioneers in any field that takes their interest.

# WHALE

**Key Words**—Precise, intellectual, spiritual

**Magical Influences**—Telepathic communication, ability to resolve personal emotional blockages, summons the aid of undines and mermaids, deep mysteries revealed

**Personality**—Whale people are usually humanitarians. They evince a high level of moral development. Whales tend to have heady, dry, or ironic senses of humor. They need to release pent-up anger through physical activity. Whales are intrigued with issues of spiritual development and enjoy philosophies that engender cross-cultural universal truths.

# WOLF

**Key Words**—Fierce, resourceful, enduring

**Magical Influences**—Grants physical and mental endurance; evokes the aid of benefic spirits, transforms negative energy

**Personality**—Wolves are determined people. Once they decide upon a particular goal or accomplishment, they will work at achieving it non-stop. They are able to endure stressful situations without feeling too put out. Wolves don't like to live in the same place for a long time; they want to experience a variety of climates and cultures. One setback of the wolf is a tendency toward gluttony.

# *animal hours list*

| Nocturnal Animals | Dusk/Dawn Animals | Diurnal Animals |
|---|---|---|
| Armadillo | Armadillo | Armadillo |
| Alligator | Badger | Alligator |
| Badger | Bat | Bear |
| Bat | Beaver | Beaver |
| Cat | Bear | Bighorn |
| Coyote | Bison | Camel |
| Dog | Bobcat | Cheetah |
| Ferret | Caribou | Chipmunk |
| Fox | Coyote | Cow |
| Gopher | Deer | Coyote |
| Hare | Elk | Deer |
| Jaguar | Ferret | Elk |
| Jack Rabbit | Fox | Ferret |
| Lemming | Gopher | Fox |
| Lynx | Hare | Gopher |
| Mink | Jack rabbit | Mink |
| Mountain Lion | Jaguar | Mole |
| Mouse | Lynx | Moose |

| Nocturnal Animals | Dusk/Dawn Animals | Diurnal Animals |
|---|---|---|
| Mole | Mole | Mountain Goat |
| Muskrat | Moose | Mouse |
| Ocelot | Mountain Lion | Musk-ox |
| Otter | Musk-ox | Otter |
| Porcupine | Muskrat | Shrew |
| Raccoon | Ocelot | Squirrel (ground) |
| Rat | Otter | Squirrel (tree) |
| Shrew | Porcupine | Wolf |
| Squirrel | Prairie Dog | Woodchuck |
| Weasel | Raccoon | |
| Wolf | Shrew | |
| | Skunk | |
| | Wolf | |

# *herbal blend index*

S teep one teaspoon of herb to one cup of boiling water. Use this infusion to do a number of things: (1) anoint yourself; (2) asperge the magic circle you are working within to draw the appropriate animal essence; (3) add it to a magical bath prior to animal work; (4) use like simmering potpourri to release its magical fragrance; (5) incorporate the herb into a fetich.

### A

Antelope—allspice, carnation
Aardvark—dill, patchouly

### B

Bear—lavender, comfrey
Boar—hyssop, basil
Bat—basil, woodruff
Beaver—blackberry juice, rose hips, sage
Bison—lavender, comfrey
Badger—comfrey, mullein
Bull—comfrey, lovage

## C

Cat—angelica, marjoram, catnip
Cougar—chamomile, angelica
Cheetah—chamomile, angelica, cowslip
Chimpanzee—chickweed, dandelion
Cobra—basil, marjoram, cinnamon
Cow—boneset, aniseed, alfalfa
Camel—chamomile, vervain, marjoram
Chinchilla—dandelion, hawthorn
Condor—marjoram, chamomile, cinquefoil

## D

Dog—chickweed, star anise, dog's grass
Dingo—chickweed, basil, dog's grass
Donkey—comfrey
Deer—lavender, mugwort, hyssop
Dove—rose buds, cinnamon
Dinosaur—cinnamon, damiana, marjoram
Duck—dandelion, lavender
Dragon—marjoram, chickweed, chamomile, cinquefoil
Dolphin—ginseng, horehound, lemon grass

## E

Elephant—chickweed, verbena, lovage
Eel—mugwort, cinnamon, damiana
Eagle—horehound, lavender, verbena

## F

Frog—cucumber, apricot, hyssop, lavender
Flamingo—lemon verbena, sage
Ferret—sage, rose hips, cowslips
Fox—cowslips, dog's grass, damiana
Fish—mugwort, hyssop
Falcon—chamomile, ginseng, cinnamon

## G

Gorilla—comfrey, chamomile, red clover
Giraffe—vervain, meadowsweet
Gazelle—marjoram, angelica
Goat—comfrey, lovage
Ground hog—lovage, lavender
Gnu—mugwort, lovage
Greyhound—dog's grass, vervain, star anise
Goose—ginger, hyssop
Gerbil—goldenseal, meadowsweet
Guinea pig—chamomile, dandelion

## H

Hog—feverfew, star anise, mugwort
Horse—comfrey, hyssop, marjoram
Hyena—barley, cinnamon
Hippo—sage, star anise, mugwort
Hare—hare's beard, lavender, basil, meadowsweet
Hamster—meadowsweet

## I

Iguana—meadowsweet, basil, cinnamon
Ibex—barley, lovage

## J

Jaguar—angelica, marjoram, cinnamon
Jackal—star anise, barley
Jack rabbit—comfrey, lavender

## K

Kangaroo—damiana, meadowsweet
Koala bear—goldenseal, chamomile

## L

Lion—chamomile, cowslips, sage
Lemming—lavender, dandelion
Lynx—sage, rose, cayenne

Lamb—lobelia, rose, balm
Lama—comfrey, lovage, damiana
Leopard—chamomile, marjoram, ginseng
Lizard—cinnamon, chamomile, lovage

## M

Moose—catnip, lovage
Muskrat—angelica, lavender
Mouse—meadowsweet, lavender
Monkey—star anise, ginger, dog's grass
Mongoose—garlic, cinnamon
Mocking bird—lavender, cinquefoil, solomon's seal
Mammoth—vervain, lovage, golden seal
Mink—chamomile, catnip
Mule—comfrey, dandelion
Mole—star anise, lovage, rose

## N

Nightingale—catnip, aniseed, rose

## O

Ostrich—rosemary, horehound, rosehips
Opossum—aniseed, mugwort
Otter—mugwort, dandelion

## P

Python—cinnamon, lovage, damiana
Pig—mullein, dandelion, goldenseal
Parrot—bayberry, rosemary, meadowsweet
Panther—sage, rosemary, dog's grass
Panda—aloes, star anise, lemon verbena

## Q

Quail—caraway, boneset, vervain

## R

Rat—hawthorn, lavender
Rodent—aniseed, lavender
Rabbit—white rose, horehound, solomon's seal
Raccoon—star anise, meadowsweet, dandelion
Rhinoceros—lovage, vervain
Ringtail cat—mugwort, ginger

## S

Snake—vervain, garlic
Salamander—hyssop, chamomile, cinnamon
Skunk—rosehips, ginger, sage
Stingray—mugwort, peach nectar, cinnamon
Seal—mugwort, dandelion
Shark—barley, aloes, cinnamon
Sheep—lobelia, balm

## T

Tasmanian devil—cayenne, eucalyptus
Turtle—lobelia, ginseng
Tortoise—ginseng, lovage, star anise
Tiger—sage, meadowsweet, solomon's seal

## U

Unicorn—meadowsweet, goldenseal

## W

Walrus—mugwort, lovage
Whale—mugwort, balm, watercress, bayberry
Wombat—camphor, lotus, fennel
Wallaby—chamomile, verbena

## Z

Zebra—verbena, rosemary

# *circle casting/banishing*

T his is meant to be a guide in creating sacred space for Witches. Feel free to experiment and change the words of power anywhere in the text, for it is best to find words of power that resonate with your own shamanic sensibilities.

## ITEMS NEEDED

- Salt
- Water
- Athame
- Red candle
- Incense
- Four candles representing the four quarters

## CIRCLE CASTING

Place your four quarter candles around the working space, one at each of the compass directions. If you are using colored candles, place the yellow one in the East, the red in the South, the blue in the West, and the green in the North. (Otherwise, use all white, since white contains all colors.)

Next place your altar[1] at the center of your circle. On it, position the salt (or Earth), on the North side of the altar; put the incense in the East; the red Fire candle in the South; and the bowl of Water in the West.

Light each of the quarter candles in turn, starting in the East and moving around clockwise or "deosil."

Return to the altar and hold your athame over the bowl of Water, saying:

> I CONSECRATE THEE, O CREATURE OF WATER, IN THE NAMES OF THE GREAT MOTHER AND THE HORNED ONE.

Hold your athame over the salt, saying:

> I CONSECRATE THEE, O CREATURE OF EARTH, IN THE NAMES OF THE GREAT MOTHER AND THE HORNED ONE.

Using your athame, scoop three small heaps of salt into the water and stir. Take the saltwater to the edge of the circle and sprinkle it all along the perimeter.

Return to the altar. Hold your athame over the Fire candle, saying:

> I CONSECRATE THEE, O CREATURE OF FIRE, IN THE NAMES OF THE GREAT MOTHER AND THE HORNED ONE.

Hold the athame over the lit incense, saying:

> I CONSECRATE THEE, O CREATURE OF AIR, IN THE NAMES OF THE GREAT MOTHER AND THE HORNED ONE.

Take the candle to the edge of the circle and take it around the perimeter. Do the same with the incense.

Next, touch yourself with the water and salt mixture at the third eye, saying:

BLESSED AM I WITH THE VIRTUES OF WATER AND EARTH.

Hold the candle and the incense near the third eye, saying:

BLESSED AM I WITH THE VIRTUES OF FIRE AND OF AIR.

Next you shall cast the formal circle, which will require all of your concentration. Stand in the East and point your athame outward to the edge of the circle. Walk clockwise, pointing the blade outward, and make one complete circle (returning to the East), saying:

I SUMMON THE CIRCLE, THE CIRCLE I SUMMON,
POWER AND PEACE AND PROTECTION WILL COME IN
AND BIND TO THE WOMB OF OUR SPIRITUAL BIRTH,
THROUGH AIR AND FIRE AND WATER AND EARTH!

Next you will invoke the powers of the elements at each of the four compass directions. Take your athame with you as you go to the Eastern quarter. Draw an invoking pentagram in the air, and say:

O SYLPHS OF THE WIND, I ASK THEE TO BLOW
AND BRING ON THY WINGS THE POWER TO KNOW!

In the Southern quarter, draw an invoking pentagram and say:

SALAMANDERS OF FIRE, I CALL THEE UNTIL
YOU BRING ON THY FLAMES THE POWER TO WILL!

In the West, draw an invoking pentagram, saying:

O UNDINES OF WATER, COME AS I DECLARE
AND BRING ON THY WAVES THE POWER TO DARE!

In the North, draw your final invoking pentagram and say:

O GNOMES OF THE EARTH, I ASK THEE ARIGHT,
BRING FROM THY MOUNTAINS THE SILENCE OF NIGHT.

Return to your altar and face East. Now you will invoke the God and Goddess. Hold your arms skyward and say:

> HEAR ME ANCIENT ONES! LADY OF THE MOON, LORD
> OF THE SUN,
> DESCEND, I PRAY, INTO THIS MY CIRCLE. BE WITH ME
> NOW TO LEND THY BLESSINGS.

This completes the casting of the circle.

## CIRCLE BANISHING

Draw a banishing pentagram in the East, saying:

> FAREWELL TO THEE, GUARDIANS OF THE EAST!
> LEAVE FROM US HERE! RETURN TO THY SPHERE!

Draw a banishing pentagram in the South, saying:

> FAREWELL TO THEE, GUARDIANS OF THE SOUTH!
> LEAVE FROM US HERE! RETURN TO THY SPHERE!

Draw a banishing pentagram in the West, saying:

> FAREWELL TO THEE, GUARDIANS OF THE WEST!
> LEAVE FROM US HERE! RETURN TO THY SPHERE!

Draw a banishing pentagram in the North, saying:

> FAREWELL TO THEE, GUARDIANS OF THE NORTH!
> LEAVE FROM US HERE! RETURN TO THY SPHERE!

Next you will banish the formal circle. Hold your athame out while standing in the East. This time, walk widdershins (counterclockwise), making one complete circle (that is, returning to the East), saying:

## AIR = EAST

INVOKING      BANISHING

## FIRE = SOUTH

INVOKING      BANISHING

## WATER = WEST

INVOKING      BANISHING

## EARTH = NORTH

INVOKING      BANISHING

## SPIRIT ACTIVE

INVOKING      BANISHING

## SPIRIT PASSIVE

INVOKING      BANISHING

*Invoking and Banishing Pentagrams*

EARTH WILL CRUMBLE MY CIRCLE,
WATER WILL CAUSE IT TO FALL,
FIRE WILL BURN WHAT'S LEFT IN THE URN,
AND THE WINDS WILL SCATTER IT ALL.

This completes the circle banishing.

## NOTE

1. The altar can be any small table or box large enough to contain the necessary tools.

# *animal incense and oils*

## SHAPESHIFTER INCENSE

- 2 parts sandlewood (preferably powdered)
- 1 part pennyroyal
- 1 part mugwort
- 1 part patchouly
- 5 drops (1 drop per part of dried herb) musk oil

## SHAPESHIFTER OIL

Mix the following into safflower oil or grapeseed oil (one ounce oil per part of dried herb):

- 1 part patchouly leaf
- 1 part pennyroyal
- 1 part mugwort

  Set the mixture on a sunny windowsill for 10 to 15 days. Strain out the herbs. To this oil add:

- 2 drops musk oil

# TOTEM SPIRIT INCENSE

- 3 parts sandlewood (preferably powdered)
- 1 parts patchouly leaf
- 2 parts cinnamon (cassia chips or powder)
- 5 drops musk oil
- 2 drops euchalyptus oil

# TOTEM SPIRIT OIL

Mix the following into safflower oil or grapeseed oil (one ounce oil per part of dried herb):

- 1 part patchouly leaf
- 1/2 part cinnamon (cassia chips)
- 1 part euchalyptus leaf

    Set the mixture on a sunny windowsill for 10 to 15 days. Strain out the herbs. To this oil add:

- 5 drops musk oil

# BLESSING OIL

This mixture is for blessing and protecting the fetich or physical Familiar as well as non-Familiar animals, and for blessing yourself before meditations.

Mix the following into safflower oil or grapeseed oil (one ounce oil per part of dried herb):

- 1 part juniper
- 1 part basil
- 1 part jasmine blossoms

Set the mixture on a sunny windowsill for 10 to 15 days. Strain out the herbs. To this oil add:

• 3 drops jasmine oil

# *animal lore from around the world*

o stop leg or stomach cramps, you should wear a bone from the head of a cod.

You can stop a dog from barking and howling by turning one of your shoes upside down.

The health of children is said to improve if you allow them to play with dogs.

If you see a dog rolling in the grass, you should expect that good luck or news from afar is coming.

It is good luck to allow a strange dog to follow you home.

A person who owns three cats, each a different color, is said to carry great luck.

A three-colored cat is said to prevents fires.

Owning a white cat brings the owner poverty.

If a spotted cat wanders into your home, it is said to be a sign of good fortune coming your way.

If you are ever followed by a black cat, you will be lucky.

It is said that if you give a cat to a friend, that will break off the friendship.

If you see a cat put its paw over its head, it means company is coming.

When the pupils of a cat's eyes are nearly closed, it shows that it is low tide. Widely opened pupils means high tide.

The time of day may be noted by observing the relative size of a cat's pupils.

A cat scratching on the front door (from the outside) means company is coming.

After a cat washes its face, be sure not to let it look at you right away—unless you want to be married soon!

Be sure to make a wish when you see a newborn calf. It is likely to come true.

Goats always seem to seek shelter before bad weather, so watch them.

When buying a horse remember this country saying:

> One white foot, buy him;
> Two white feet, try him;
> Three white feet, try another day;
> Four white feet, give him away.

Saying "white horse" seven times will help you find a lost article.

Never give a pig away. You'll be giving away your luck!

If when starting a journey, you see a rabbit cross your path, it will be a safe journey.

If a squirrel runs across the road in front of you, it means good luck and wealth are going to be yours soon.

Buzzards take a long time in between wing beats. So if you see a lone buzzard, make a wish before he flaps his wings and your wish will come true.

Seeing the shadow of a buzzard on the ground without seeing the buzzard means company is coming.

To stop an owl from making its night calls, tie a knot in a blue handkerchief.

A rooster crowing early in the morning means good weather is ahead for that day.

A rooster crowing late at night means a storm is coming.

A rooster crowing in front of your door means news from a distance is coming.

A rooster crowing in the early part of the night means there is news coming fast.

To keep evil away from your house, throw the egg of a white hen over your right shoulder toward the front door of the house.

When you see a crow for the first time in a new year, observe its flight—that will indicate the distance you will travel that year. If the crow just sits there, it means no journey; if it flies out of sight, it means you'll take a very long journey.

Here is an ancient folk rhyme about crows and what their flock size indicates:

> One crow, sorrow,
> Two crows, mirth,

> Three crows, a wedding,
> Four crows, birth.

It was believed not long ago that crows could talk.

Make a wish when you hear the first call of a dove on the Spring Equinox and the wish will come true.

What you are doing when you hear the first whippoorwill, you will do all the year long.

It is good luck to have a wren build a nest near your home (preferably in your yard).

It is good luck to have a wild bird come into your house.

When a mockingbird flies over the house of someone single, that person will be married within a year.

If a dark bird sits on your windowsill, you should expect luck.

You will recieve a letter from a loved one if you see a red bird cross a road you are traveling.

In some parts of the United States, it was believed that moles were incarnations of old people who had passed on.

Black hellbore herb is used in the blessing of domestic animals. Mix the herb into water at dawn, strain, and bless the animals by sprinkling them.

Red clover holds energy thought to be benevolent to animals. Utilize this herb in the healing of domestic animals.

Whatever occupation one has when he hears the frogs croak for the first time in the spring, will be one's occupation for the entire year.

Here is a saying about seeing spiders that fortells your immediate future:

> If you see a black one, it means sad news;
> If you see a brown one, it means glad news;
> If you see a white one, it means good luck in all views.

Make a wish when you see a spider spinning a web and the wish will come true.

If you see a brown spider crawling around on any clothes in your closet, don't brush it away! The spider means you will be getting new clothes.

A bee flying into the house means a stranger is coming.

If you say "mumbly up" repeatedly over an anthill, the ants will come up out of the hole. Saying "mumbly down" makes the ants go back down.

Never talk to snakes: snakes are thought to be deaf.

It is lucky to have a snake live in, near, or under your house.

# bibliography

Beane, Wendell, and William Doty, eds. *Myths, Rites and Symbols: A Mircea Eliade Reader.* New York: Harper/Colophon Books, 1976.

Beryl, Paul. *The Master Book of Herbalism.* Custer, Washington: Phoenix Publishing, 1984.

Boguet, Henrey. *An Examen of Witches.* Great Britain: John Rodker, 1929. Reprint. New York: Barnes & Nobles, 1971.

Campbell, Joseph. *The Hero With a Thousand Faces.* New Jersey: Princeton University Press, 1973.

Campbell, Joseph, and Bill Moyers. *The Power of Myth.* New York: Doubleday, 1988.

Castleden, Rodney. *The Stonehenge People: An exploration of Life in Neolithic Britain 4700-2000 B.C.* London: Routledge Kegan Paul, 1987.

Cory, Hans. *African Figurines: Their Ceremonial Use in Puberty Rites in Tanganika,* London: Faber and Faber, 1956.

Crocker, Jon Christopher. *Vital Souls.* Tucson: University of Arizona Press, 1985.

Cunningham, Scott. *The Complete Book of Incense, Oils and Brews.* St. Paul, Minnesota: Llewellyn Publications, 1989.

Czaja, Michael. *Gods of Myth and Stone.* New York: Weatherhill, 1974.

Czaplicka, Marie Antoinette. *Aboriginal Siberia.* London: Oxford University Press, 1969.

Day, Harvey. *Occult Illustrated Dictionary.* London: Oxford University Press, 1976.

Dioszegi, Vilmos, and M. Hoppal, eds. *Shamanism in Siberia.* Budapest: Akadëmiai Kiadö, 1978.

Dioszegi, Vilmos. *Tracing Shamans In Siberia.* Oosterhout: Anthropological Publications, 1968.

Dorsey, George A. *The Dwamish Indian Spirit Boat and Its Use.* Bulletin, University of Pennsylvania, University Museum, 3.4, 1902.

Dukore, Bernard F. *Dramatic Theory and Criticism.* San Francisco: Duke Reinhart and Winston Inc., 1974.

Eisler, Riane. *The Chalice and the Blade.* San Francisco: Harper and Row, 1987.

Eliade, Mircea. *Shamanism: Archaic Techniques of Ecstasy.* Trans. Willard R. Trask. New York: Pantheon Books, 1964.

Elkin, A.P. *Aboriginal Men of High Degree.* St. Lucia, Queensland: University of Queensland Press, 1977.

Faraday, Ann. *The Dream Game.* New York: Harper & Row, 1974.

Farrar, Janet and Stewart. *The Witches' God.* Custer, Washington: Phoenix Publishing, 1989.

—————. *The Witches' Way.* London: Robert Hale, 1984.

Frazer, James G. *The Golden Bough,* vol. I. 1890. Reprint. New York: Avenel Books, 1981.

————————. *Totemism and Exogamy*, vol. II. Cambridge: Messrs. Macmillan and Co. Ltd., 1968.

Ford, Patrick, ed. *The Mabinogi and other Medieval and Welsh Tales*. Berkeley: University of California Press, 1977.

Gantz, Jeffrey, trans. *The Mabinogion*. London: Penguin Books, 1976.

Getty, Adele. *Goddess, Mother of Living Nature*. London: Thames and Hudson Ltd., 1990.

Giffard, George. *Dialogue Concerning Witches*, vol. 8. London: Percey Society, 1843.

Gimbutas, Marija. *Gods and Goddesses of Old Europe*. London: Thames and Hudson, Ltd., 1974.

————————. *The Language of the Goddess*. San Francisco: Harper-Collins, 1989.

Grey, Eden. *The Tarot Revealed*. New York: Signet Books, 1969.

Grim, John A. *The Shaman: Patterns of Siberian and Ojibway Healing*. Norman: University of Oklahoma Press, 1983.

Halphide, Alvin C. *Mind and Body*. Chicago: Monarch Book Company, 1899.

Harner, Michael J. *Hallucinogens and Shamanism*. New York: Oxford University Press, 1973.

————————. *The Way of the Shaman*. New York: Bantam, 1980.

Hart, Mickey. *Drumming at the Edge of Magic*. New York: HarperCollins Publishers, 1990.

Highwater, Jamake. *The Primal Mind: Vision and Reality in Indian America*. New York: Meridian Books, 1982.

Judith, Anodea. *Wheels of Life: A Users Guide to the Chakra System*. St. Paul, Minnesota: Llewellyn Publications, 1990.

Kurtz, Ron, and Hector Prestera, M.D. *The Body Reveals.* New York: Harper and Row, 1976.

Leland, Charles G. *Aradia, Gospel of the Witches.* 1890. Reprint. Washington: Phoenix Publishing, 1990.

Long, Max Freedom. *Secret Science Behind Miracles.* Marina Del Rey, CA: DeVorss, 1983.

Malandro, Loretta A., Larry Barker, and Deborah Barker. *Nonverbal Communication.* 2nd ed. New York: Random House, 1989.

Matthews, John. *Taliesin; Shamanism and the Bardic Mysteries in Britain and Ireland.* Hammersmith, England: Aquarian Press, 1991.

Mellaart, James. *Catal Hüyük.* New York: McGraw Hill, 1967.

Merriam, Alan P. *The Anthropology of Music.* Chicago: Northwestern University Press, 1964.

Murray, Margaret. *The Witch-Cult in Western Europe.* 1921. Reprint. London: Oxford University Press, 1962.

——————. *The God of the Witches.* 1931. Reprint. New York: Oxford University Press, 1970.

Ornstein, Robert. *The Psychology of Consciousness.* New York: Viking Penguin Inc., 1986.

Potts, Thomas. *Pott's Discovery of Witches in the County of Lancaster,* vol. 6. 1613. Reprint. Manchester: Chetham Society, 1745.

Rivers, W.H.R. *Medicine, Magic and Religion.* 1924. Reprint. New York: Harcourt and Brace, 1979.

Robbins, Russel Hope. *Encyclopedia of Witchcraft and Demonology.* New York: Crown Publishers, 1912.

Roheim, Geza. *The Eternal Ones of the Dream.* New York: International Universities Press, 1945.

Roth, Gabrielle. *Maps to Ecstasy.* San Rafael, California: New World Library, 1989.

Rutherford, Ward. *Celtic Mythology.* New York: Sterling Publishing Co., 1990.

Schlesier, Karl H. *The Wolves of Heaven.* Trans. *Die Wölfe des Himmels.* Norman: University of Oklahoma Press, 1987.

Scot, Reginald. *The Discoverie of Witchcraft.* London, 1584. Reprint. Carbondale, IL: Southern Illinois University Press, 1964.

Sjöo, Monica, and Barbara Mor. *The Great Cosmic Mother.* San Francisco: Harper Collins, 1987.

Sproul, Barbara C. *Primal Myths: Creation Myths Around the World.* San Francisco: HarperCollins Publishers, 1991.

Smith, Steven R. *Wylundt's Book of Incense.* York Beach, Maine: Samuel Weiser, Inc., 1989.

Starhawk. *The Spiral Dance: A Rebirth of the Ancient Religion of the Great Goddess.* New York: HarperCollins Publishers, 1989.

——————. *Truth or Dare.* San Francisco: Harper and Row, 1987.

Steiger, Brad. *Kahuna Magic.* Glouchester, MA: Para Research, Inc., 1981.

Tyler, Hamilton A. *Pueblo Animals and Myths.* Norman: University of Oklahoma Press, 1964.

Underhill, Evelyn. *Mysticism: A study in the nature and development of man's spiritual consciousness.* New York: E.P. Dutton and Co., 1911.

Valiente, Doreen. *An ABC of Witchcraft.* New York: St. Martin's Press, 1973.

Vizenor, Gerald. *Summer in the Spring: Lyric Poems of the Ojibway.* Minneapolis: Nodin Press, 1981.

Walker, Barbara G. *The Women's Encyclopedia of Myths and Secrets.* San Francisco: Harper and Row, 1983.

Webster, John. *The Displaying of Supposed Witchcraft.* London: F.M., 1677.

# index

## STAY IN TOUCH

On the following pages you will find listed, with their current prices, some of the books now available on related subjects. Your book dealer stocks most of these and will stock new titles in the Llewellyn series as they become available. We urge your patronage.

To obtain our full catalog, to keep informed about new titles as they are released and to benefit from informative articles and helpful news, you are invited to write for our bi-monthly news magazine/catalog, *Llewellyn's New Worlds of Mind and Spirit*. A sample copy is free, and it will continue coming to you at no cost as long as you are an active mail customer. Or you may subscribe for just $10.00 in U.S.A. and Canada ($20.00 overseas, first class mail). Many bookstores also have *New Worlds* available to their customers. Ask for it.

Stay in touch! In *New Worlds'* pages you will find news and features about new books, tapes and services, announcements of meetings and seminars, articles helpful to our readers, news of authors, products and services, special money-making opportunities, and much more.

### *Llewellyn's New Worlds of Mind and Spirit*
### P.O. Box 64383-439, St. Paul, MN 55164-0383, U.S.A.
### * * *
### TO ORDER BOOKS AND TAPES

If your book dealer does not have the books described on the following pages readily available, you may order them direct from the publisher by sending full price in U.S. funds, plus $3.00 for postage and handling for orders *under* $10.00; $4.00 for orders *over* $10.00. There are no postage and handling charges for orders over $50.00. Postage and handling rates are subject to change. UPS Delivery: We ship UPS whenever possible. Delivery guaranteed. Provide your street address as UPS does not deliver to P.O. Boxes. UPS to Canada requires a $50.00 minimum order. Allow 4-6 weeks for delivery. Orders outside the U.S.A. and Canada: Airmail—add retail price of book; add $5.00 for each non-book item (tapes, etc.); add $1.00 per item for surface mail.

### FOR GROUP STUDY AND PURCHASE

Because there is a great deal of interest in group discussion and study of the subject matter of this book, we feel that we should encourage the adoption and use of this particular book by such groups by offering a special quantity price to group leaders or agents.

Our Special Quantity Price for a minimum order of five copies of *The Once Unknown Familiar* is $30.00 cash-with-order. This price includes postage and handling within the United States. Minnesota residents must add 6.5% sales tax. For additional quantities, please order in multiples of five. For Canadian and foreign orders, add postage and handling charges as above. Credit card (VISA, MasterCard, American Express) orders are accepted. Charge card orders only ($15.00 minimum order) may be phoned in free within the U.S.A. or Canada by dialing 1-800-THE-MOON. For customer service, call 1-612-291-1970. Mail orders to:

### LLEWELLYN PUBLICATIONS
### P.O. Box 64383-439, St. Paul, MN 55164-0383, U.S.A.

*Prices subject to change without notice.*

## SHAMANISM AND THE ESOTERIC TRADITION
### by Angelique S. Cook & G.A. Hawk

Recharge and enhance your magical practice by returning to the *source* of the entire esoteric tradition—the shamanism of the ancient hunters and gatherers.

Whether you're involved in yoga, divination, or ritual magic, *Shamanism and the Esoteric Tradition* introduces you to the fundamental neo-shamanic techniques that produce immediate results. Shamanic practice is a tremendous aid in self-healing and personal growth. It also produces euphoria by releasing beta-endorphins, an effective antidote against depression.

The enormously powerful techniques presented here include inner journeys to find a power animal and teacher, past-life regression, healing methods, and journeys to help the dead. Gradually and properly used, shamanic power helps you generate positive synchronicities that can alter so-called "chance" life events, and enhance personal satisfaction, freedom and wholeness.

**0-87542-325-6, 224 pgs., 6 x 9, illus., index, softcover**                **$12.95**


## ANIMAL-SPEAK
### The Spiritual & Magical Powers of Creatures Great & Small
### by Ted Andrews

The animal world has much to teach us. Some are experts at survival and adaptation, some never get cancer, some embody strength and courage while others exude playfulness. Animals remind us of the potential we can unfold, but before we can learn from them, we must first be able to speak with them.

Now, for perhaps the first time ever, myth and fact are combined in a manner that will teach you how to speak and understand the language of the animals in your life. *Animal-Speak* helps you meet and work with animals as totems and spirits—by learning the language of their behaviors within the physical world. It provides techniques for reading signs and omens in nature so you can open to higher perceptions and even prophecy. It reveals the hidden, mythical and realistic roles of 45 animals, 60 birds, 8 insects and 6 reptiles.

Animals will become a part of you, revealing to you the majesty and divine in all life. They will restore your childlike wonder of the world and strengthen your belief in magic, dreams and possibilities.

**0-87542-028-1, 400 pgs., 7 x 10, illus., photos, softcover**                **$16.00**

## DANCE OF POWER
### A Shamanic Journey
### by Dr. Susan Gregg

Join Dr. Susan Gregg on her fascinating, real-life journey to find her soul. This is the story of her shamanic apprenticeship with a man named Miguel, a Mexican-Indian Shaman, or "Nagual." As you live the author's personal experiences, you have the opportunity to take a quantum leap along the path toward personal freedom, toward finding your true self, and grasping the ultimate personal freedom—the freedom to choose moment by moment what you want to experience.

Here, in a warm and genuine style, Dr. Gregg details her studies with Miguel, her travel to other realms, and her initiations by fire and water into the life of a "warrior." If you want to understand how you create your own reality—and how you may be wasting energy by resisting change or trying to understand the unknowable—take the enlightening path of the Nagual. Practical exercises at the end of each chapter give you the tools to embark upon your own spiritual quest.

Learn about another way of being ... *Dance of Power* can change your life, if you let it.
**0-87542-247-0, 5 1/4 x 8, illus., photos, softbound          $12.00**


## SHAMANISM AND THE MYSTERY LINES
### Ley Lines, Spirit Paths, Shape-Shifting & Out-of-Body Travel
### by Paul Devereux

This book will take you across archaic landscapes, into contact with spiritual traditions as old as the human central nervous system and into the deepest recesses of the human psyche. Explore the mystery surrounding "ley lines": stone rows, prehistoric linear earthwork, and straight tracks in archaic landscapes around the world. Why would the ancients, without the wheel or horse, want such broad and exact roads? Why the apparent obsession with straightness? Why the parallel sections?

Are they energy lines? Traders' tracks? For those who have definite ideas as to what a ley line is, be prepared for a surprise ... and a possible shift in your beliefs about this intriguing phenomenon.

The theory put forth and proved in *Shamanism and the Mystery Lines* is startling: that all ancient landscape lines—whether physical manifestations as created by the Amerindians or conceptual as in the case of Feng shui—are in essence *spirit lines*. And underlying the concept of spirit and straightness is a deep, universal experience yielded by the human central nervous system: that of shamanic magical flight—or the out-of-body experience. This explanation is as simple and direct as the lines themselves ... flight is the straight way over land.
**0-87542-189-X, 240 pgs., 6 x 9, illus., softcover          $12.95**

## THE COMPLETE BOOK OF INCENSE, OILS AND BREWS
### by Scott Cunningham

For centuries the composition of incenses, the blending of oils, and the mixing of herbs have been used by people to create positive changes in their lives. With this book, the curtains of secrecy have been drawn back, providing you with practical, easy-to-understand information that will allow you to practice these methods of magical cookery.

Scott Cunningham, world-famous expert on magical herbalism, first published *The Magic of Incense, Oils and Brews* in 1986. *The Complete Book of Incense, Oils and Brews* is a revised and expanded version of that book. Scott took readers' suggestions from the first edition and added more than 100 new formulas. Every page has been clarified and rewritten, and new chapters have been added.

There is no special, costly equipment to buy, and ingredients are usually easy to find. The book includes detailed information on a wide variety of herbs, sources for purchasing ingredients, substitutions for hard-to-find herbs, a glossary, and a chapter on creating your own magical recipes.

**0-87542-128-8, 288 pgs., 6 x 9, illus., softcover** **$12.95**

## BUCKLAND'S COMPLETE BOOK OF WITCHCRAFT
### by Raymond Buckland

Here is the most complete resource to the study and practice of modern, non-denominational Wicca. This is a lavishly illustrated, self-study course for the solitary or group. Included are rituals; exercises for developing psychic talents; information on all major "sects" of the Craft; sections on tools, beliefs, dreams, meditations, divination, herbal lore, healing, ritual clothing and much, much more. This book unites theory and practice into a comprehensive course designed to help you develop into a practicing Witch, one of the "Wise Ones." It is written by Ray Buckland, a very famous and respected authority on Witchcraft who first came public with the Old Religion in the United States. Large format with workbook-type exercises, profusely illustrated and full of music and chants. Takes you from A to Z in the study of Witchcraft.

Never before has so much information on the Craft of the Wise been collected in one place. Traditionally, there are three degrees of advancement in most Wiccan traditions. When you have completed studying this book, you will be the equivalent of a Third-Degree Witch. Even those who have practiced Wicca for years find useful information in this book, and many covens are using this for their textbook. If you want to become a Witch, or if you merely want to find out what Witchcraft is really about, you will find no better book than this.

**0-87542-050-8, 272 pgs., 8 1/2 x 11, illus., softcover** **$14.95**

## WICCA
### A Guide for the Solitary Practitioner
### by Scott Cunningham

*Wicca* is a book of life, and how to live magically, spiritually, and wholly attuned with Nature. It is a book of sense and common sense, not only about Magick, but about religion and one of the most critical issues of today: how to achieve the much needed and wholesome relationship with out Earth. Cunningham presents Wicca as it is today: a gentle, Earth-oriented religion dedicated to the Goddess and God. This book fulfills a need for a practical guide to solitary Wicca—a need which no previous book has fulfilled.

Here is a positive, practical introduction to the religion of Wicca, designed so that any interested person can learn to practice the religion alone, anywhere in the world. It presents Wicca honestly and clearly, without the pseudo-history that permeates other books. It shows that Wicca is a vital, satisfying part of twentieth century life.

This book presents the theory and practice of Wicca from an individual's perspective. The section on the Standing Stones Book of Shadows contains solitary rituals for the Esbats and Sabbats. This book, based on the author's nearly two decades of Wiccan practice, presents an eclectic picture of various aspects of this religion. Exercises designed to develop magical proficiency, a self-dedication ritual, herb, crystal and rune magic, recipes for Sabbat feasts, are included in this excellent book.

**0-87542-118-0, 240 pgs., 6 x 9, illus., softcover** **$9.95**


## LLEWELLYN'S MAGICAL ALMANAC

This enchanting yearly guide for Pagans has become a faithful friend to magical people the world over. It's chock full of articles, usable monthly calendars, magical advice and captivating artwork. What's more, its value lasts beyond the year—the captivating articles on a variety of magical subjects make this a long-cherished keepsake for decades to come.

**288 pgs., 5 1/4 x 8, softcover** **State year** **$7.95**

## WHEELS OF LIFE
### A User's Guide to the Chakra System
### by Anodea Judith

An instruction manual for owning and operating the inner gears that run the machinery of our lives. Written in a practical, down-to-earth style, this fully illustrated book will take the reader on a journey through aspects of consciousness, from the bodily instincts of survival to the processing of deep thoughts.

Discover this ancient metaphysical system under the new light of popular Western metaphors: quantum physics, elemental magick, Kabbalah, physical exercises, poetic meditations, and visionary art. Learn how to open these centers in yourself, and see how the chakras shed light on the present world crises we face today. And learn what you can do about it!

This book will be a vital resource for: Magicians, Witches, Pagans, Mystics, Yoga Practitioners, Martial Arts people, Psychologists, Medical people, and all those who are concerned with holistic growth techniques.

The modern picture of the Chakras was introduced to the West largely in the context of Hatha and Kundalini Yoga and through the Theosophical writings of Leadbeater and Besant. But the Chakra system is equally innate to Western Magick: all psychic development, spiritual growth, and practical attainment is fully dependent upon the opening of the Chakras!

0-87542-320-5, 544 pgs., 6 x 9, illus., softcover                    **$14.95**


## IN THE SHADOW OF THE SHAMAN
### Connecting with Self, Nature & Spirit
### by Amber Wolfe

Presented in what the author calls a "cookbook shamanism" style, this book shares recipes, ingredients, and methods of preparation for experiencing some very ancient wisdoms: wisdoms of Native American and Wiccan traditions, as well as contributions from other philosophies of Nature as they are used in the shamanic way. Wheels, the circle, totems, shields, directions, divinations, spells, care of sacred tools and meditations are all discussed. Wolfe encourages us to feel confident and free to use her methods to cook up something new, completely on our own. This blending of ancient formulas and personal methods represents what Ms. Wolfe calls Aquarian Shamanism.

*In the Shadow of the Shaman* is designed to communicate in the most practical, direct ways possible, so that the wisdom and the energy may be shared for the benefits of all. Whatever your system or tradition, you will find this to be a valuable book, a resource, a friend, a gentle guide and support on your journey. Dancing in the shadow of the shaman, you will find new dimensions of Spirit.

0-87542-888-6, 384 pgs., 6 x 9, illus., softcover                    **$12.95**

## MAGICKAL DANCE
### Your Body as an Instrument of Power
### by Ted Andrews

Choreograph your own evolution through one of the most powerful forms of magickal ritual: Dance. When you let your inner spirit express itself through movement, you can fire your vitality, revive depleted energies, awaken individual creativity and transcend your usual perceptions.

Directed physical movement creates electrical changes in the body that create shifts in consciousness. It links the hemispheres of the brain, joining the rational and the intuitive to create balance, healing, strength and psychic energy.

This book describes and illustrates over 20 dance and other magickal movements and postures. Learn to shapeshift through dance, dance your prayers into manifestation, align with the planets through movement, activate and raise the kundalini, create group harmony and power, and much more. Anyone who can move any part of the body can perform magical movement. No formal dance training is required.
0-87542-004-4, 224 pgs., 6 x 9, illus., photos, softcover            **$9.95**


## DREAM ALCHEMY
### Shaping Our Dreams to Transform Our Lives
### by Ted Andrews

What humanity is rediscovering is that what we dream can become real. Learning to shift the dream to reality and the reality to dream—to walk the thread of life between the worlds—to become a shapeshifter, a dreamwalker, is available to all. We have the potential to stimulate dream awareness for greater insight and fulfillment, higher inspiration and ultimately even controlled out-of-body experiences. It is all part of the alchemical process of the soul.

Through the use of our ancient myths and tales, we can initiate a process of dream alchemy. Through control of the dream state and its energies, we are put in touch with realities and energies that can open us to greater productivity during our waking hours. Learn to alter sleep conditions and increase dream activity through the use of herbs, fragrances, crystals, flower essences, totems, talismans and mandalas.

For those just opening to the psychic and spiritual realms, this is one of the safest and easiest ways to bridge your consciousness to higher realms.
0-897542-017-6, 264 pgs., 6 x 9, illus., softcover            **$12.95**

## WITCHCRAFT TODAY: BOOK THREE
### Witchcraft & Shamanism
### edited by Chas S. Clifton

This book is a compelling and honest examination of shamanic techniques (both classical and neo-) as they are being practiced in Neopagan Witchcraft in the 1990s. Shamanism is a natural adjunct to the ritualistic and magical practice of many covens and solitary Pagans. In this ground-breaking volume, you will discover how others have integrated techniques such as trance journeys, soul retrieval, and altered states of consciousness.

Discover how shamanic ideas influenced Greek philosophers, Platonists, Pythagoreans and Gnostics ... learn how evidence from the old witch trials suggests that at least some Europeans may have practiced shamanic journeying in the past ... incorporate caves for ritual and inner journeys, both literally and in visualization ... find out who is out there retrieving souls and curing elfshot ... compare the guided visualizations common to modern magickal practice with the neo-shamanic journey ... learn how spirit contacts are made, how guides are perceived and what "worlds" they reside in ... and much more.

1-56718-150-3, 304 pgs., 5 ¼ x 8, photos, softbound                                  $9.95


## TO RIDE A SILVER BROOMSTICK
### New Generation Witchcraft
### by Silver RavenWolf

Throughout the world there is a new generation of Witches —people practicing or wishing to practice the craft on their own, without an in-the-flesh magickal support group. *To Ride a Silver Broomstick* speaks to those people, presenting them with both the science and religion of Witchcraft, allowing them to become active participants while growing at their own pace. It is ideal for anyone: male or female, young or old, those familiar with Witchcraft, and those totally new to the subject and unsure of how to get started.

Full of the author's warmth, humor and personal anecdotes, *To Ride a Silver Broomstick* leads you step-by-step through the various lessons with exercises and journal writing assignments. This is the complete Witchcraft 101, teaching you to celebrate the Sabbats, deal with coming out of the broom closet, choose a magickal name, visualize the Goddess and God, meditate, design a sacred space, acquire magickal tools, design and perform rituals, network, spell cast, perform color and candle magick, divination, healing, telepathy, psychometry, astral projection, and much, much more.

0-87542-791-X, 320 pgs., 7 x 10, illus., softcover                                  $14.95

*Prices subject to change without notice.*

## LIVING WICCA
### A Further Guide for the Solitary Practitioner
### Scott Cunningham

*Living Wicca* is the long-awaited sequel to Scott Cunningham's wildly successful *Wicca: a Guide for the Solitary Practitioner*. This new book is for those who have made the conscious decision to bring their Wiccan spirituality into their everyday lives. It provides solitary practitioners with the tools and added insights that will enable them to blaze their own spiritual paths—to become their own high priests and priestesses.

*Living Wicca* takes a philosophical look at the questions, practices, and differences within Witchcraft. It covers the various tools of learning available to the practitioner, the importance of secrecy in one's practice, guidelines to performing ritual when ill, magical names, initiation, and the Mysteries. It discusses the benefits of daily prayer and meditation, making offerings to the gods, how to develop a prayerful attitude, and how to perform Wiccan rites when away from home or in emergency situations.

Unlike any other book on the subject, *Living Wicca* is a step-by-step guide to creating your own Wiccan tradition and personal vision of the gods, designing your personal ritual and symbols, developing your own book of shadows, and truly living your Craft.

0-87542-184-9, 208 pgs., 6 x 9, illus., softcover                    **$10.00**


## SPELL CRAFTS
### Creating Magical Objects
### Scott Cunningham & David Harrington

Since early times, crafts have been intimately linked with spirituality. When a woman carefully shaped a water jar from the clay she'd gathered from a river bank, she was performing a spiritual practice. When crafts were used to create objects intended for ritual or that symbolized the Divine, the connection between the craftsperson and divinity grew more intense. Today, handcrafts can still be more than a pastime—they can be rites of power and honor; a religious ritual. After all, hands were our first magical tools.

*Spell Crafts* is a modern guide to creating physical objects for the attainment of specific magical goals. It is far different from magic books that explain how to use purchased magical tools. You will learn how to fashion spell brooms, weave wheat, dip candles, sculpt clay, mix herbs, bead sacred symbols and much more, for a variety of purposes. Whatever your craft, you will experience the natural process of moving energy from within yourself (or within natural objects) to create positive change.

0-87542-185-7, 224 pgs., 5 1/4 x 8, illus., photos                    **$10.00**


*Prices subject to change without notice.*

## ROBIN WOOD TAROT DECK
**created and illustrated by Robin Wood**
**Instructions by Robin Wood and Michael Short**
Tap into the wisdom of your subconscious with one of the most beautiful Tarot decks on the market today! Reminiscent of the Rider-Waite deck, the Robin Wood Tarot is flavored with nature imagery and luminous energies that will enchant you and the querent. Even the novice reader will find these cards easy and enjoyable to interpret.

Radiant and rich, these cards were illustrated with a unique technique that brings out the resplendent color of the prismacolor pencils. The shining strength of this Tarot deck lies in its depiction of the Minor Arcana. Unlike other Minor Arcana decks, this one springs to pulsating life. The cards are printed in quality card stock and boxed complete with instruction booklet, which provides the upright and reversed meanings of each card, as well as three basic card layouts. Beautiful and brilliant, the Robin Wood Tarot is a must-have deck!
**0-87542-894-0, boxed set: 78-cards with booklet** $19.95

## THE WITCHES TAROT DECK
**by Ellen Cannon Reed and Martin Cannon**
Author Ellen Cannon Reed has created the first Tarot deck specifically for Pagans and Wiccans. Reed, herself a Wiccan High Priestess, developed The Witches Tarot as a way to teach the truths of the Hebrew Kabbalah from a clear and distinctly Pagan point of view. Changes include a Horned One in place of the traditional Devil, a High Priest in place of the old Hierophant, and a Seeker in place of the Hermit. Comes complete with an instruction booklet that tells you what the cards mean and explains how to use the "Celtic Cross" and "Four Seasons" layouts. The gorgeous, detailed paintings by Martin Cannon make this a true combination of new beauty and ancient symbolism. Even many non-pagans have reported excellent results with the cards and appreciate their colorful and timeless beauty.
**0-87542-669-7, Boxed set: 78 full-color cards with booklet** $17.95

*Prices subject to change without notice.*

## THE GODDESS SEKHMET
### Psychospiritual Exercises of the Fifth Way
### by Robert Masters, Ph.D.

Here is the story of the ancient goddess Sekhmet, a form of the Great Mother related to the creative and destructive power of the Sun. Most importantly, this book presents Sekhmet as an archetypal force, guiding the reader into a positive direct experience of the Living Goddess, her teachings and life-transforming rituals.

As a result of Dr. Masters' direct encounter with Sekhmet in a series of telepathic trance states, he has received the teachings of the sacred books of Sekhmet that were lost, pillaged from the temples and destroyed by unbelievers. This is a book of the reconstructed scriptures and spiritual disciplines that will open its readers to the mysteries, supernatural powers, and mind-body-spirit transformations of Sekhmet. Half of *The Goddess Sekhmet* consists of Psychospiritual Exercises, which are techniques that can be practiced primarily as psychological exercises and as a way to improve the health and functioning of the brain and nervous system. By doing the exercises, the reader will increase the awareness of, and ability to use, more latent human potentials.

0-87542-485-6, 256 pgs., 6 x 9, photos, softcover                                  $12.95
0-87542-495-3, 256 pgs., 6 x 9, photos, hardcover                                  $22.95


## ANCIENT WAYS
### Reclaiming the Pagan Tradition
### by Pauline Campanelli, illus. by Dan Campanelli

*Ancient Ways* is filled with magick and ritual that you can perform every day to capture the spirit of the seasons. It focuses on the celebration of the Sabbats of the Old Religion by giving you practical things to do while anticipating the sabbat rites, and helping you harness the magical energy for weeks afterward. The wealth of seasonal rituals and charms are drawn from ancient sources but are easily performed with materials readily available.

Learn how to look into your previous lives at Yule . . . at Beltane, discover the places where you are most likely to see faeries . . . make special jewelry to wear for your Lammas Celebrations . . . for the special animals in your life, paint a charm of protection at Midsummer.

Most Pagans and Wiccans feel that the Sabbat rituals are all too brief and wish for the magick to linger on. *Ancient Ways* can help you reclaim your own traditions and heighten the feeling of magick.

0-87542-090-7, 256 pgs., 7 x 10, illus., softcover                                  $12.95

## A WITCH'S GUIDE TO FAERY FOLK
### Reclaiming Our Working Relationship with Invisible Helpers
### by Edain McCoy

All over the world, from time immemorial, people have reported encounters with a race of tiny people who are neither human nor deity, who live both inside and outside of the solid human world. Now, for the first time, a book reclaims that lost, rich heritage of working with faery folk that our Pagan ancestors took as a matter of course. Learn to work with and worship with faeries in a mutually beneficial way. Practice rituals and spells in which faeries can participate, and discover tips to help facilitate faery contact.

Even among believers in faeries, the active role of these astral-world creatures in ritual and magical workings has been virtually eliminated. This book discusses the existence of the astral plane, the personality of various faery types and faery mythology. It even teaches you how to create your own thought-form faery beings.

Whether you are a Pagan or simply wish to venerate nature and commune with these creatures of the wild, *A Witch's Guide to Faery Folk* is an invaluable aid in this exciting exploration.

ISBN: 0-87542-733-2, 340 pgs., 6 x 9, 60 illus., 17 photos $12.95


## CIRCLE OF THE COSMIC MUSE
### by Maria Kay Simms

*Circle of the Cosmic Muse* integrates Wiccan ritual practice and astrological knowledge. It contains complete rituals—based closely on astrological symbolism—for one full year of Esbats and Sabbats, plus rituals for special occasions such as weddings, funerals, blessing and naming children. For astrologers who seek to bring the energy of planetary cycles into a personal experience, the rituals are beautifully constructed and easy to follow. For the Wiccan looking to blend ritual practice into the "cosmic" scheme of things, the astrological information is presented in an easy-to-understand and direct fashion.

Additionally, this book is a detailed "how-to" for setting up and running a Wiccan circle, and it offers a unique perspective on the philosophy and ethical framework of Wiccan practice. There are many paths to truth, many ways to seek the Goddess and God within. With this book, you have an example of one path, one system, that you can use in part or as a whole, just as you choose.

ISBN: 1-56718-656-4, 496 pgs., 6 x 9, illus., softbound $15.95